Positive Planning for Rural Houses

Published by
Irish Rural Dwellers Association

Cumann Lucht Conaithe na Tuaithe

Is cultúr tuaithe í cultúr na héireann. Tá ceól, litríocht, drámaíocht agus cluichí na tíre suite ins na ceanntracha tuaithe. Tá an saol tradisiúnta bunúsach seo i mbaol anois toisc an córas gallda pleannála atá i bfeidm sa tír le blianta beag anuas. Tá an córas pleannála seo bunaithe ar riactanaisí na breathaine atá éagsúil in iomlán o riactanaisí na éireann.

Buníodh cumann lucht conaithe na tuaithe breis is blian ó shoin chun córas gaelach a chur in ionad an coras mí daonfhlaitheach atá ann faoi láthair. Tá an-tacíocht faighte againn le blian anuas ó ceann ceann na tíre. Cheana féin tá tacaíocht faighte againn ón rialtas agus tá gach dóchas againn go néireiogh linn ár cuspóiri a bhaint amach. Tá tosach maith déanta agus le brú agus comhoibriú ó muintir na tuaithe ar fad beidh an bua againn.

Cathal MacGabhann,
Cathaoirleach

ISBN 0-9547926-0-2

Published by Irish Rural Dwellers Association

Irish Rural Dwellers Association would like to thank the following for their assistance in the production of this publication;
Main Photography: Dave Dakin of Image Photography, Kilbaha Kilrush, County Clare
Design: Optic Nerve Design Group, www.OpticNerve.ie
Editor: Jim Connolly

All contributors; Dr. Seamus Caulfield, Dr. Jerry Cowley, Cathal MacCabhann, Risteard O'Domhnall, Sean O'Donoghue, T. C. Lynch, Michael Healy Rae and the IAVI who kindly supplied articles, essays and previously published material without charge.

Contents

Introduction

IRDA and Planning

Introduction

Rural Ireland has always been well served with voluntary associations which reflect the rich cultural fabric of society. Farming, fishing, social, economic, sporting, cultural and virtually all aspects of life have attracted people to commit their personal time and energy to the advancement of voluntary community work.

Pre 1963, when the first planning acts were enacted in modern Ireland, planning, as such, was rarely an issue in rural life; consequently the subject wasn't very high on the list of priorities of voluntary organisations dealing with their own specific, dedicated agendas.

However, the huge changes that have occurred in Ireland since the sixties—some of which have resulted in previously unknown levels of income and opportunities for the general run of people—have rocketed planning issues to centre stage. There is now a constant battle being waged between conflicting forces; on the one hand, the needs and aspirations of new generations demanding the right to build houses, while on the other hand, a whole raft of rules, regulations, environmental groups, journalists, planning authorities, Officials, the National Spatial Strategy, Regional County and Local Area Development Plans etc. are all widely perceived to be conspiring to thwart peoples rights and choices in one form or another. That is not to say that no planning is being given for rural housing—indeed it is self evident to anyone driving around Ireland that we are now in an age of house building, both in urban and rural areas, that has not been seen since the famine, when the population was almost double what it is now.

However, in this context, it is important to note that the house sizes and styles of bygone days, which in general reflected the abject poverty and deprivation of the ordinary people of Ireland, are totally unsuited to modern families or the legitimate expectations of people in the 21st Century.

All national architecture, by its very nature, reflects the social, cultural and economic life of different ages and peoples. In Ireland, we still have the magnificent Georgian houses reflecting the wealth and privilege of previous ruling classes. We also have the remains of the tiny bohans—little more than heaps of stones, sods and thatch in which the majority lived.

Romantic ideology and legitimate archaeological concerns aside, there is no way that the rural landscape of Ireland can be fossilised or preserved in a 19th Century mode while at the same time, tens of thousands of tax paying citizens are denied the basic right of building houses for their families of types and styles which are practical and affordable, which meet modern standards of health, safety and insulation and which inevitably are bigger and brighter than those built in the past. Built of a mixture of modern as well as traditional materials, methods and designs, the houses of today proclaim to the world that for the first time in history the average Irish citizen can live in his or her home to a standard of comfort heretofore the exclusive right of the wealthy.

This is one of the major social advances in Irish history of which the nation should be justly proud.

Differences of opinion have always existed in society on the subject of architectural styles, designs, use of materials etc. A modern society must strike a balance in favour of democracy and social justice when imposing restrictions on housing. The views of elitist establishment groups who believe that they alone carry the torch of superior wisdom from generation to generation and consequently have the right to impose these views by way of rules, regulations and restrictions on the general public represents a situation which can no longer be tolerated in a modern democracy.

These establishment views, with corresponding pressures on the general public to conform, are a hangover from the past. The finer points of art, literature, music, design, architecture etc. even personal morality were considered to be way above the heads of the great unwashed and by and large, the masses needed to be told what was good for them by their betters.

Whether these views emanate today from private professional bodies such as Architects Associations and an Taisce or from statutory sources such as Local Authorities, the Arts Council, the Planning Institute, The Royal Town Planning Institute, Universities or otherwise, this authoritarian approach must end.

That a conflict exists between planners and the general public is evident to all, but the contestants are so unevenly matched that natural justice is often the chief casualty in planning applications.

In the present situation, the constitutional right of the ordinary citizen to build a home, to sell a site or otherwise to develop their property is completely outmatched by the weight and strength of those authorities who are determined to control and restrict that right and who do so to such an extent that, in the end the constitutional right has become meaningless.

Control is exercised on a divide and conquer basis. Individual applications for rural houses have no connection with others of the same kind. Therefore, if an application is refused by the planning authority and again by An Bord Pleanala, the individual has no choice but to give up and lick his or her wounds. (The High Court is rarely an affordable option). There are many cases now of people leaving Ireland because they cannot get permission to build.

But because most rural dwellers and others wishing to live in rural areas believe strongly that basic human rights' issues are at stake, it became clear that a united front would be essential to defend and reassert these rights.

Many of the leaders of farming, cultural and other rural organisations report that planning issues are constantly to the fore of people's worries. However, none of these organisations have a brief to deal specifically with these issues. It was felt that with the growing importance of planning in peoples lives, a new organisation representing all rural dwellers, which would focus mainly on planning issues, was needed.

Hence the arrival on the scene of the IRDA. The original organising committee not alone represented the leadership of many of Irelands largest rural organisations, but was also guided and inspired by some outstanding individuals in Irish life, whose public stand for democracy and justice in planning is a matter of record. These included Dr. Seamus Caulfield, Professor of Archaeology, Cathal MacGabhann, retired CEO of Udaras na Gaeltachta, Senator Labhras O Murchu, Dr. Jerry Cowley, TD., Marian Harkin, TD, and many others.

Depending entirely on voluntary commitment the IRDA was launched in May 2002 and has had a massively successful first year with support groups and county branches being formed from Donegal to Mayo to Caherciveen to Wexford and many counties in between. There is an elected National Executive Committee and the IRDA is Registered as a Company Limited by Guarantee.

Some General Points:

Traditional Stone Housing:

Maintaining old houses is a labour of love and quite an expensive exercise. It is also a minority interest which holds very little if any relevance to the huge demands for housing today.

Local authorities, who are the only housing authorities in the land and as such have to comply with building regulations, fire risks, Health and Safety issues etc, generally do not include the restoration and upgrading of old solid wall houses as part of their housing programmes.

Lack of damp courses, under floor membranes, radon barriers, ceiling heights, window sizes, cold, dampness, room sizes etc. etc. all add up to an impossible situation except for the dedicated enthusiast.

Legal Action:

One of the objectives of the IRDA will be to explore the possibility that legal actions will be taken on constitutional questions—even if the organisation itself has to take a case. This may well become an option if new laws promised on Class Actions in Ireland are enacted.

One such legal question might be planning refusals based on visually vulnerable or similar landscape reasons. *See Appendix (CAAS Environmental Services Report 1997)*

An Taisce:

A brief reference to An Taisce's policies for rural areas. To confine planning permissions for rural houses to those with a connection to the land / agriculture is the most philosophically barren, culturally impoverished, anti rural community, racist and basically unconstitutional policy that has been attempted in Ireland. It is utterly opposed by the IRDA. A third of the population of Ireland live in dispersed village communities. Less that 10% are involved in farming.

If an Taisce have their way, we will have tiny, unsustainable, one class only rural communities. Gone will be the housing opportunities for factory workers, professionals, artists, craft-workers, poets, musicians, writers, merchants and all the other rich mix of people who go to make up culturally diverse and vibrant rural communities.

In this booklet, the IRDA introduce a long overdue balance to the debate by presenting the perspective of people who live in the countryside. This booklet challenges many of the 'facts', assumptions and statements made by planning authorities and An Taisce on rural housing issues.

Foreword

By Jim Connolly

Acting Secretary IRDA

The production of this booklet, like the foundation of the IRDA itself, is a serious response by large numbers of deeply concerned Irish citizens to the simplistic—almost one dimensional—approach being pursued by the planning regime, to urbanise the country.

Thousands of years of tradition are being thrown out as having no relevance and cultural aspects of rural community life count for nothing in this head long drive for high density living.

The blind eye is being turned to the obvious and inevitable downsides of urbanisation like traffic congestion, impossible house prices, rising crime, pollution, noise, stress, drugs etc. while the equally obvious upsides to the quality of life of rural living are attacked and denigrated as being unsustainable.

But the rural people have now said enough is enough. The brakes are on and bureaucrats will experience an ever increasing resistance from the taxpayers who pay their wages, to being herded like animals into towns and villages against their wishes.

The most extraordinary and incomprehensible aspect to the current situation is that the Irish Government in its stated policies and in statements by individual Ministers are clearly concerned for the survival and development of our rural culture and way of life and recognise that this cannot be achieved without people continuing to live in the countryside, while on the other hand, the entire bureaucratic planning regime supported by An Taisce, The Royal Institute of Architects, The Royal Town Planning Institute and An Bord Pleanala pursue a completely opposite agenda and couldn't care less about Government policy.

From one end of Ireland to the other, ordinary people and large numbers of frustrated elected representatives are calling on the Government to make the planning regime comply, but to no avail. Notwithstanding the fact that planning philosophies at work are imported ones and largely UK influenced, or that large numbers of professional planners are non-nationals who have no knowledge or understanding of Irish culture and history and who are not obliged to undergo any education in these aspects, the fact that the Government is unable or unwilling to control their day to day activities has left the human and constitutional rights of citizens at their mercy and the very future of a populated countryside at risk.

Our elected County Councillors should be in control, but clearly, in many cases, they are not. As far as planning goes, bureaucracy rules and citizens suffer.

The formation of the IRDA in May 2002 has been fully justified insofar as it has been accepted by the Department of the Environment as a body which speaks for large numbers of rural dwellers on planning issues relating to rural housing. We were invited to meet senior officials preparing the long awaited Rural Housing Guidelines and have done so on two occasions. We also met Minister Martin Cullen on the same issues.

The following text was circulated to officials outlining the background context prior to our meeting with the Minister.

Setting the context
- "Rural Development and the well being of rural community is a public good" (Government White Paper)
- Sustaining human life requires ongoing new developments. Development is vital for survival.
- Virtually all new developments from the most basic to the largest and most sophisticated have both upsides and downsides for humanity. At no stage has a point been reached—even in the most advanced societies—where a perfect balance was achieved resulting in an end to new development.

Assessing New Developments
Quality of life:
One yardstick for assessing the beneficial aspects of major new developments might be the added value to the quality of life of the greatest number of people. This can be quantified over time by comparing average life expectancy, infant mortality, general health and other concrete statistics.

Housing
In Ireland concerted efforts at inner city slum clearances and the provision by local authorities of basic but better quality housing with clean water and sanitation was one major development which brought quantifiable positive results. These will be further improved if poverty and social exclusion can be eliminated.

Rural Housing
Most farmers and other rural dwellers had no piped water of flushed toilets until the 1960s. Small subsistance farmers lived in cold, damp, thatched, stone houses. However 'romantic' and idyllic looking to urban tourists, life for the occupants was hard, lacking in basic amenities and often unhealthy. To the hundreds of thousands who had to emigrate, these houses symbolised a life of abject poverty.

Its only within the past forty years or so, that some grants were introduced for septic tanks, new roofs and other improvements.

New Age
Today, however, Ireland has entered upon a new age of prosperity and building unthought of even twenty years ago. This most welcome development will see tens of thousands of modern, high quality houses being added to the national housing stock. The majority are being built in urban areas where two thirds of the population live, but in justice, the other third who live in scattered rural communities must also benefit from new housing.

In considering rural housing, other aspects, such as national rural characteristics, culture, language, traditions and social justice must be taken into account.

Visual Impact:
However, the visual impact of so much new building is certainly changing the face of Ireland. Apart from rural houses, the growth of urban housing estates, apartment and office blocks, factories, hotels, retail centres etc. as well as massive motorways and flyovers—all contribute hugely to the new look.

To many, this inescapable visual change is a seriously negative factor. But in the light of the many positive, national interest implications of this new age, to single out rural houses for special condemnation mainly on one single issue ie. landscape (which is subjective in any event) is a superficial, one dimensional approach which has the potential to destroy rural community life if it is allowed to continue to dominate planning.

Rural families have a right to aspire to houses which meet modern standards of health, safety and comfort. Such houses are necessarily bigger and quite different in general appearance from the older, mostly sub standard houses. New home owners are proud to express their new found economic freedom, creativity and modernity in bright colours, landscaping and high quality upkeep.

Design

Only a small proportion of wealthy people can commission individual architect designed houses. Most other people have little say over the design of modern houses. Many building components which were once hand made are now mass produced. Regional differences are gone. Just like our clothes, cars, phones and most other aspects of modern life, the houses being built in Ireland today are international in virtually all respects.

Whether one likes or dislikes this fact of life, it must be made clear that modern housing is not a wicked invention by rural people (no more than holiday homes are) and the fact that we are endlessly being maglined and pilloried by journalists with ignorant, defamatory phrases such as "bungalow blitz" and "aesthetic blight" has reached a point where injustice in planning is now a running sore in rural Ireland.

Footnote

In this selective thumbnail sketch of the situation it would be wrong to conclude that aspects such as heritage, proper planning, archaeology, scenic beauty, water pollution etc. are not taken into serious consideration by the IRDA. When journalists write that the IRDA are at loggerheads with conservationists, we argue that rural dwellers are the real conservationists who care for the countryside on a daily basis. This will become tragically clear in terms of neglect, overgrowth, dereliction, desertification and the end of rural tourism if rural communities are wiped out by enforced policies of urbanisation and villigisation.

The IRDA is a voluntary, non-profit, non-political and non-sectarian organisation. It is registered as a Company Limited by Guarantee and will be seeking charitable status.

The main aim is:

"To unite all rural dwellers and people of goodwill towards rural Ireland and in the context of peaceful, multi cultural co-existence in the common cause of ensuring, by legal and constitutional means, the growth and maintenance of a vibrant, populated countryside in the traditional Irish forms of baile fearann or dispersed village, sraid bhaile or street village and the clachan or nucleated (clustered village)".

Its success to date is due entirely to the unstinting and huge voluntary commitment by individuals throughout the country—many of whom are considerably out of pocket as a result. The individual aspect of taking responsibility for, not alone the future of the IRDA, but for the future of our countryside cannot be over emphasised. Within the IRDA there should never be a 'them and us' situation between elected officers and everybody else. To paraphrase John F. Kennedy—it is not a matter of what 'they should be doing' nor indeed 'what we should be doing' but rather the question must be 'what should I be doing to make things happen'.

This booklet covers a wide range of topics relating to life in general and the ever increasing dominance of bureaucracy and planning in controlling personal freedom and human rights. The range of topics is essential because so many vital areas of life are sidelined, ignored and civil rights abused by planners in the narrow and restrictive concept of planning based primarily on land use strategies.

The contributors to this booklet come from a cross section of Irish life with only a very few having qualifications in planning. Therefore the booklet does not purport to be a text book on planning. Rather it is ordinary people putting planning in context in the life of the country. People and community take priority at all times —planning is the servant, not the master.

It is vital that the views of the people who are directly affected by planning be catalogued and listened to.

Finally, the IRDA is a democratic organisation and while a number of essays and different sections of the book carry the names of individual contributors, they are all presented in the same spirit ie. to stimulate thought and discussion.

Allowances must be made for differences in points of view or emphasis on various topics within the organisation.

Historical Settlement Patterns

Dispersed villages: The breakdown of the 42% of the total population who are classified as rural is 8% in small towns and nucleated street villages and 34% who live in communities of dispersed villages. The tradition of the settled dispersed community goes back at least five and a half thousand years in Ireland, four times longer than the tradition of nucleated settlement in towns or street villages.

- The native culture of Ireland, as in other Celtic regions which were not part of the Roman Empire or Feudal Europe, is mainly rural. Our cities and towns were founded by Norse and Norman invaders.
- Our Irish and Anglo Irish literature, traditions and customs are mainly rural.
- Our traditional settlement pattern was based on the dispersed village, as compared with the feudal or provincial settlement pattern of other countries.
- Ireland is the only country in Europe which has suffered a (very large) fall in population during the past 150 years.

The rural population has declined in the 26 counties from 6.5 million in 1845 to 1.5 million in 2000 whereas urban population has risen from 1 million to 2.4 million. If the present planning regime continues with increasing urbanisation the rural population will be decimated in the next 25 years with the continued industrialisation of agriculture.

Rural Ireland will be reduced to a green desert. Our culture, traditions and history are largely rural (not necessarily agricultural) and the urban / rural mix is the key to our national identity.

Because of the planners headlong drive for urbanisation and their suppression of rural buildings we have the highest annual price increase in the world for houses (London Economist 8/3/03) which is making affordable housing out of reach for most young couples.

Because of our unique decline in population between 1845 and 1971, we have the lowest population density in the European Union, South of the Arctic Circle—eg. 54 per sq.km by comparison with England 390, the Netherlands 388, Belgium 336, Germany 230 etc. This means that the settlement pattern which is being imposed by the planners and which may be appropriate in densely populated countries need not apply in Ireland.

Irish Planning History

By T.C. Lynch, (Kerry Branch IRDA)

Chapter Two

What Does Planning Mean?

Planning is to think out before hand how something is to be made or done. A scheme of action carefully contrived to achieve a given aim, effect, purpose or goal, used in all different ways, by individuals, businesses, the state and state Authorities. An example of planning by the state and state agencies is the preparation of the national spatial strategy by the government and the county development plans being prepared by each council at the moment, known as "Town Planning"

Town Planning

"Town Planning" means two different things. Firstly it means making a complete design lay-out in advance for a new town or extension of a town, and the location of its streets, parks, and buildings etc. Secondly its more usual meaning is public control by the state or local councils, over the design development and arrangement of buildings and land use. It is now referred to as "Town & Country Planning"

Town & Country Planning

"Town & Country Planning" because it applies to areas much wider than towns and includes the countryside around and between the towns, does not only involve the control of land use development, but also the identification of regional economic and social factors must be considered when development policies are decided. This type of planning is quite recent and modern, while "Town Planning" has gone on during many periods of history in different parts of the world. Town planning by the Cretans, Greeks, and Macedonians in the eastern Mediterranean, goes back three thousand years. Alexander the Great who lived until 323 B.C. founded many cities in the countries he conquered and then occupied them with his soldiers. The Romans when they invaded Western Europe and England, planned and built new cities on sites taken by force, they occupied them with their armies, and used them as their military strongholds, and as a result they did not have to bother about the wishes of the people sent to live in them.

Towns built in France, England, and Wales in the time of Edward 1st (1239-1307) had a strong roman influence, and some of those influences and ideas were carried over into the towns built by the rulers in the 17th, 18th, and 19th centuries. Organised planning of Towns however has been the exception rather than the rule in the thousands of towns scattered throughout the world, and this also applies to the towns in Ireland. The towns in Ireland grew from a few houses built at a cross roads, or the junction of a few roads coming together. The use of land and the placing of buildings were not planned and the towns grew in a haphazard fashion. The reason for this is that throughout history Agriculture took precedence over towns and cities.

The land belonged in small parcels to many owners, each farming the parcel he owned. With the passing of time and the innovative developments of the relevant period, trades, handicraft, and manufacturing began and more people moved into the villages, which grew into towns and the towns grew into cities. Each person built his own house, shop, or workshop to suit himself or his work, on the plot of ground he owned or could buy from another person. There was very little to stop a person from putting his building where he wanted, or from using it or enlarging it as he chose. The positioning of the buildings was not important and it was quiet common to find buildings protruding into the streets. It was the exception to find a cobbled or concrete footpath in a village and in some towns. The corner houses at the cross roads of the villages or towns had a slip stone at the corner of the building to protect the building from the horse drawn cart while rounding the corner.

Possibly the very first restraint or limit on what people could do with their house or building was when they had enlarged the structure to the extent that it covered the plot of ground they owned and they were stopped from extending into the public roadway. They then built up higher and in some instances extended the upper stories out over the footpath or road. In some towns the buildings were so high and close together that they cut off each other's light and resulted in disputes over ancient lighting. Overcrowding, dark rooms, lack of sanitary facilities, and proper services caused a lot of problems. Towns continued to grow and people changed the use of their buildings: houses were changed to shops, workshops and little factories, and the gardens were built over. Rows of houses back to back with little or no gardens were built in some towns, resulting in towns that were open and pleasant when they were small, became dirty, disorganised, and untidy as they grew larger. Even towns that were relatively well planned for their time became confused and out-of-date as a result of the increase in the population, the gradual building, rebuilding, traffic, and other changes. For instance, in towns where the old streets still remain, traffic has increased to such an extent that they are no longer adequate to serve their purpose.

It is because of all these difficulties that town planning, in the second meaning described at the beginning of this article, has come in to use. Laws now govern, and control the positioning and use of buildings in the towns, and the open countryside. The initial introduction of planning was associated with municipal engineering, and town extensions, and suburbs were better laid out, with wide streets, houses not too near the road edge, and reasonable space between the houses. This procedure was later adopted for parts of towns already built, where old buildings were being knocked down and replaced. It allowed for the widening of streets, provision of open space, and the reduction of overcrowding.

This planning by law began late in the 19th century in continental Europe, notably Germany and Sweden. In England planning was introduced in 1909, and the entire country became subject to planning regulations in 1947.

In 1968 they decided to review the system and carried out a survey, and found that the facts were continually changing in relation to the people, their houses, the work they did, how they got to their work, the existing roads and the amount of traffic on them, the shopping areas, schools, churches, places of entertainment, public buildings, parks, the quality of farm land and what it produced, and many other relevant facts. The only reference of note on planning in this country until the introduction of the Local Government (Planning and Development) Act, 1963 was a Government white paper in 1947 which stated that it estimated there would be need for 100,000 new houses by the beginning of the 1960s to replace the old and dangerous buildings in the country, the majority of which were in Dublin.

Irish Town Planning

Irish Town Planning now known as "Town & Country planning" was first introduced to this country under the Local Government (Planning and Development) Act, 1963.

Prior to the introduction of planning, it was the exception to have plans prepared for any structure, or development, other than those undertaken by the State, Church, Hotels, Factories, and large Georgian Houses.

At the time of its introduction to this country, the country side was inhabited mainly by rural families, with farms varying in size, and the farm houses dispersed in each town land, hence the description "the dispersed village".

Services in the countryside were provided by the sporadic shop, primary school, creamery, and petrol pump, to cater for the needs of the local community, made up of the people from a group of town lands in the immediate area. Transport was provided by a daily bus service six days a week between towns in areas where the train service had been removed during the 1950's. A postman from the local post office delivered the mail daily to the people on his bicycle. The primary school children walked to the nearby school, and the older children walked or cycled to the secondary school a distance of up to twenty kilometres from where they lived.

Large areas of the countryside were still without electricity or a public water supply (Television was in its infancy with only one station—R.T.E One). Very few Primary or Secondary roads were to design standard, county roads were substandard, very rough, un-surfaced, and narrow. As a result travel was slow and difficult.

Only towns and some villages had a public water supply, and the same applied to sewerage facilities. Water supplies in the open countryside were mostly from wells, streams, or rain water storage tanks constructed from building material, and replenished with rain water from the roof of the house. Usually the sewerage system was provided by earth closet, chemical closet, or cesspool with drain connections.

The standard of living accommodation was very basic, and it was not unusual to find houses without flush toilets, or bathrooms, in the towns and countryside. The farm labourer's cottage with a floor area between 55sq M and 75sq M built by the Councils in the open countryside was constructed with a three thousand gallon rainwater storage tank, and had a chemical closet for toilet facilities. The area of the site was one acre and ten perches 0.430Ha. This system prevailed until the introduction of serviced housing in the countryside in 1965.

Serviced Housing

When serviced housing was introduced to this country in 1965 the site area for a rural cottage was reduced from 1a 0r 10p (0.430Ha) to a quarter of an acre (0.101 Ha.) This area is also the standard site area adopted for planning purposes and applied to private and grant aided houses of 1245sq ft (115Msq) in the rural areas. This site area has been increased to one third of an acre (0.135Ha) where a public water supply is available and half an acre (0.202Ha) where water is supplied from a well or similar source. This is consistent with the original site area for rural cottages and for Government grant aided houses, and bears little relevance to the size of houses being constructed today, which are much larger than those envisaged when planning was introduced in 1963.

Site percolation tests in accordance with N/1/65 were performed for rural cottages since the introduction of serviced housing in nineteen hundred sixty five. Private and grant aided housing was exempt from this procedure until the introduction of percolation testing in 1991, as a result of the report by the National Standards Authority of Ireland (NSAI) on septic tank systems, and its recommendations for domestic effluent treatment and disposal from a single dwelling house (NSAI standard recommendations S.R.6.1991). This might account for recent concerns and complaints made by environmental groups about pollution from septic tanks. On the introduction of serviced housing to the countryside people availed of Government grants for the provision of bathrooms, septic tanks, and the construction of new houses.

In the early to mid sixties a policy to complete rural electrification was undertaken by the E.S.B. The councils improved and surface dressed the county roads, and the Government made grants available for the provision of group water schemes. These infrastructural improvements helped to transform the standard and quality of life for the people living in the rural areas, and helped people to a quality of life never before experienced in the countryside

National Spatial Strategy

The national spatial strategy is a plan initiated by the Government and decides on the regional development of the country, its resources, industrial base and future development potential. An expert consulting firm is engaged by the Government and prepares the plan after research and consultation with various bodies and the general public.

Development Plan

The development plan also known as town planning is prepared by each County Council, City Corporation, and Urban District Council, for their respective areas. The various councils after consultation, discussions, and general debate with interested organisations and the general public, decide on the policy, strategy and regulations for all forms of development within their respective areas. When the development plan (known as the peoples plan) is prepared by the officials it is then put before the elected members of the council for ratification as a statutory document.

Planning Administration

The administration of planning is in turmoil at present with a lot of scepticism in the planning process as a result of the revelations from the Planning Tribunal into irregularities in the planning process in the Dublin Area. It has to be remembered that Dublin is only one of Twenty Six Counties, and when applicants in other Counties are met with the bias and partiality shown by some officers when arriving at their decisions in relation to planning permission, it creates unease about the credibility of the planning system. The lack of uniformity in planning decisions by planning officers, and their failure to admit and rectify errors in their assessment of planning applications, resulting in a refusal of planning permission to the applicant, invariably leads to resentment by those affected. Some as a result, may challenge the decision to refuse permission by the Planning Authority and proceed with having a section four motion voted on to have permission granted by the Council.

This leads to objections to An Bord Pleanala from third parties, in particular members of "An Taisce". While some members of that organisation must be complimented for the part they played in exposing the corruption in the Dublin planning system, it must be stated that the objective of the organisation in the other twenty five counties is to prohibit the construction of single rural houses in the open countryside for the indigenous people, and instead move the rural population into estates developed by speculators in nearby towns and villages. Members of "An Taisce" have been known to object to single rural houses for the indigenous people in the countryside, up to a distance of 50kms from where they themselves live, while being supportive of large scale developments by speculators on un serviced land on the outskirts of towns where they reside.

It must be stressed that there are no known records of objections made by "An Taisce" members against planning permissions granted to state officials, officials of finance houses, or business people who wish to move to the countryside up to thirty kilometres or more from towns where those people work, and have permanent homes, to sites in the countryside, owned by financial institutions and developed by speculators. In some cases the sites have been hoarded for over fifteen years and outline permission has been re-issued periodically by the Planning Authority. In some cases sites have changed owners four and five times without ever being built on. This practice denies people the right to choose where they want to live, and the right of the rural people to live in their ancestral hinterland.

In most cases an objection from a member of "An Taisce" and the decisions arrived at by the planning officers are preferred by An Bord Pleanala when making their decision to refuse planning permission. In some cases it has been found that An Bord Pleanala base their grounds for refusing permission on the recommendation of their inspectors. When it is pointed out to the Bord with factual evidence that the report of their inspector which is identical to the report of the planning officer is incorrect, they justify their decision to refuse permission by shifting the goal posts, and stating that "they do not have to base their reason for refusing permission on the recommendation of their inspector, and that once they make their decision their jurisdiction is spent, and that anyway it is the function of the Planning Authority to grant or refuse planning permission".

Decisions arrived at in this way are a great injustice to the person who has been refused planning permission, as the only avenue left open to them is to seek a judicial review, which is not an option, because of the period of time and prohibitive costs involved.

It has been alleged that planning policy and administration infringes on the rights of the individual and could be contrary to the constitution of Ireland (Bunreacht na hÉireann). Article 44-1 of the constitution acknowledges that Ireland is a Christian Country and as such, one of its principal values in accordance with its corporal works of mercy, is to harbour the homeless, in other words to provide shelter for its

people. Article 43-1 acknowledges that the individual, by virtue of their rational being has the natural right, antecedent to positive law to the private ownership of external goods, land, property etc. It guarantees to pass no law attempting to abolish the right of private ownership, or the general right to transfer, bequeath, and inherit property, unless regulated by the principles of social justice, and the exigencies of the common good.

It further ensures under article 45 that the State shall strive to promote the welfare of the whole people by securing and protecting as effectively as it may a social order in which justice and charity shall inform all the institutions of the national life. That the citizens (all of whom men and women equally have the right to an adequate means of livelihood) may through their occupations find the means of making reasonable provision for their domestic needs, and there may be established on the land in economic security as many families as in the circumstances shall be practicable. The State further pledges itself to safeguard with especial care the economic interests of the weaker sections of the community and where necessary to contribute to the support of the infirm, the orphan, and the aged.

There is a widely held perception that there has been a constant erosion and infringement of above rights since the introduction of "Planning" to this country in 1963. The present national development plan for the Country, and the Co. Development Plans confirm this perception.

The National Plan shows no concern for people living in peripheral areas, such as the plight of the small farmer, the fishing community, and the general fraternity that make up a rural community. The lands occupied and worked by the small farmer with the few dairy cows to help sustain himself and his family in the past are still there, but the cows are no more in those areas. The enormous costs involved in implementing the new requirements for milk production by the small farmers, has made it unviable for them, and forced them out of their livelihoods. With proper planning and policy put in place to organise those farmers into work groups or mini co-ops, (using their land holdings as shares), their individual costs and overheads could have been unified and thereby reduced. This would mean they could still be working their farms today in the same industry, and develop add on products to help supplement their incomes.

The National Development Plan shows very little sympathy for the West, and South coast areas of the Country, and makes no attempt to invigorate, develop, or expand industrial bases in counties such as Donegal, Mayo, Galway, Clare, or Kerry. Instead industrial development has been regionalised with the emphasis on zoning of economic nodes and corridors in central areas of the country. Infrastructural development will be confined to those areas also.

The County Development plans have introduced restrictions and denial of the rights of the people also with the introduction of special amenity areas, secondary amenity areas, rural settlement policy, and residency clause. The settlement policy does not allow the individual to choose where they wish to live, while the residency clause imposed on property owners in the countryside is selective and does not allow the same rights as those enjoyed by people in the urban areas.

The building levies proposed at the moment on people providing their own first time homes are penal, and should not be introduced. Some of the people affected by the levies are industrial workers who generate the revenue for providing the State services, and are engaged in insecure employment. Those people who are showing the initiative to house themselves, and are borrowing large sums of money to provide their own home, thereby taking the burden off the State, should be encouraged, and helped, and not penalised by the introduction of levies, and the denial of planning permission.

The change in administration of the planning system, changed what was a quasi judicial system based on impartiality, integrity, and objectivity, into a free for all, where a formal application for planning permission once received by the planning authority became informal, and exposed to subjectivity and partiality. It is not unusual to find personal letters on file to planning officers from speculators and their agents in relation to planning applications, and the permission attaching to those files changed in favour of the applicant without the proper procedures being followed. It has been argued that the status and personality of the applicant is of greater influence in arriving at a decision than the merits or demerits of the proposal. It is not uncommon to find planning officers exceeding the powers afforded them as planning administrators and compromising both themselves and the Authority for whom they work by their actions. The introduction of planning officers from other Countries to administer the Planning System, without any knowledge of the history, language, settlement policy, and culture, has led to all sorts of problems, including the lack of uniformity of decisions.

When genuine concerns are expressed and complaints made to the management of the Councils where indiscretions have occurred, no action has been taken by management to address the problem, or to discipline the officers involved. This has led to a situation where planning officers feel they can exceed the authority afforded them by the development plans, totally disregard the rights of the individual, the elected representative and the people, and dispense the type of planning they wish to dictate.

Recommendations

As a result of the problems encountered in the administration of the planning service over the past number of years, and the fallout from the planning tribunal, it is essential to have safeguards put in place to restore credibility, and confidence in the service, and the following is recommended.

(1) Fractious objections from people living more than a few hundred metres from a proposed development should not be entertained, unless it is established that the objection is in the common good, this would reduce the gross interference and denial of both civil and constitutional rights suffered by people as a result of objections from people who do not live in the immediate area of the development, or in some cases even know the location of the development.

(2) Some form of review body, Ombudsman, or Arbitrator, should exist between the Planning Authority, and the referral of an appeal or objection to An Bord Pleanala. This would help to address the lack of uniformity in decisions and help to eliminate any errors or deviance from the regulations by the planning officers when arriving at their decisions. It would also help in the control of problems in relation to third party objections and failure of people to adhere to the planning attaching to a development.

(3) Hoarding of sites by speculators to drive up the price should be discouraged, as the planning attaching to their land contributes to the refusal of permission to those people in need of housing in the vicinity who apply for permission to build on their own land. Sites with planning permission attaching for more than three years without being built on should be revoked and not renewed to the same applicant. There are sites still available today for which planning permission was granted initially fourteen years hence, and some of those sites have changed owners four and five times since permission was initially granted without they being built on. At the present time it is not unusual to find applications being processed for some of those sites to have planning re issued for a further period of five years. The stated need by the applicants is that they wish to sell them.

(4) Relativity should be introduced to Planning, where the site area is relative to the size of the proposed structure, with a minimum site area of one third of an acre (0.135Ha) for a standard structure of 1245Sq Feet (115sqM). The site frontage should also be relative to the major axis of the structure, (perhaps twice the major axis). This would reduce the affect of ribbon development. The access avenue to the structure should be of a curved design, and not of regular formation as at present. This would allow for screening of the structure from the public roadway. The building line from the roadway should be relative to the size and bulk of the building with minimum distances in line with the importance of the roadway. This would help to eliminate the streetscape effect.

Buildings should be designed to accommodate the contours of a site, and blend in with the landscape, and not the contours and landscape defaced to accommodate the structure as at present. Innovation, Artistic, and Architectural creativity, should be encouraged and accommodated, as each period is depicted by the Architecture and building's. The Architectural heritage we treasure and enjoy today (Stately Mansions, Round Towers, and Castles) would never have been built if the planning restrictions we have today were in force at their inception.

Planning and the Rights of the Individual

Chapter Three

Quality of life / Constitutional rights:

On the assumption that every law abiding citizen has a right to pursue the quality of life of their choice, the question arises if planning laws can force a person to endure or accept without choice, a quality of life which is anathema to them and may even, in their judgement, be injurious to their health and safety. In this context, surely it is one of the most basic human rights that no third party opinion can legally supersede the right of a law abiding individual to make the ultimate choice as to what circumstances represent a threat to their health and safety. An example of this would be the written agreement required of a hospital patient before surgery can be performed.

In other aspects of modern life, entire communities can feel their quality of life and health are threatened for example, by radiation from masts, or pollution from dumps etc., but if they take legal action to defend their rights, the problem very often is to prove that the perceived danger is real and quantifiable. In cases where they lose the legal action, some individuals may have the option to leave the area if they remain convinced of the danger.

Making one other assumption in this regard, it is probably true to say that a persons quality of life is hugely influenced (but not exclusively) by the immediate environment and general circumstances in which they live. Examples from both ends of the spectrum could be life in an idyllic rural setting on one hand, compared to life in a terraced house in an urban area of high unemployment on the other. Many other examples could be used to illustrate the same point.

In the majority of cases, choosing the ideal quality of life, boils down to a matter of money. Rich people at the top of the scale can generally live where and how they wish. They have a vast range of options and choices. Poor people at the bottom of the scale generally have no choices at all. They are lucky if they secure a local authority house (given the long waiting lists) and have little or no say in the type of environment in which it is located.

Tens of thousands of Irish citizens have suffered appalling deprivation in terms of quality of life over several generations because of this lack of choice and, in spite of the recent Celtic Tiger, there is little evidence that things are getting any better for those caught in the poverty trap.

While acknowledging the depth of guilt and shame that applies to Irish society in general for allowing this degradingly poor quality of life to continue from generation to generation, we must also acknowledge that the focus of the struggle for justice in planning applies mainly to people in employment or to those who can otherwise aspire to building the house of their dreams in the location of their choice.

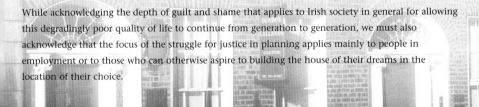

The large segment of the population who are neither super rich nor caught in the poverty trap have every legitimate right to pursue the quality of life of their choice. Very few may achieve their ultimate dream house in the right location, but given that they are taxpaying citizens whose energies and skills contribute hugely to our economic success, they are demanding recognition of their constitutional rights in the pursuit of their housing aspirations.

Towns and villages:

Apart from the cost factor, few difficulties face those whose ideal quality of life is to buy or build in towns or street villages. In general, planning is very supportive of their lifestyle choices. But for a great many people quality of life means space. Spacious rooms to live in, space around the house, space for children to play in safety, space for a garden to enjoy closeness with nature, space for family pets, space for privacy, space for security, space for sheds or workshops for hobbies, space for personal / enterprise development. Even the most superficial study of social history will show that this relationship between quality of life and space is evident in the large houses and surrounds enjoyed by the affluent classes everywhere in the world. It is a perfectly natural and easily understood phenomenon.

To many who can afford it the ideal lifestyle is a house in a large walled garden in the suburbs of a town or city. By today's standards, such a property could be priced in millions of Euro. For the majority who seek space for living, property at these prices is not an option. In Ireland, people from a rural or indeed an urban background seeking their personal space may compare what towns and villages have to offer by comparison with life in the traditional dispersed village.

We have said that for many, quality of life is directly related to the amount of personal space available for living. This is not a new phenomenon - the difference now is that a far greater proportion of the population (in Ireland) can aspire to gaining this level of personal space than in previous generations because of the more even and equitable distribution of wealth. Education, options and choices are all part of the general mix that goes with economic development.

It goes without saying that people who choose to live in the countryside as part of the traditional dispersed village or town land get all the space that one could wish. Houses are generally built on half-acre sites and neighbouring houses may be some distance away scattered in all directions. Some country areas are reasonably thickly populated in this manner and many other areas are either very thinly populated or have no houses at all. It is worth reminding ourselves that Ireland in the beginning of the 21st century is by far the least sparsely populated country in Europe (south of the Arctic Circle). Ireland also has the lowest housing density per head of the population. Overall, outside of our cities and towns there is an almost unlimited amount of space available for spacious living for the citizens of Ireland even allowing for increases in population which might someday reach the EU average.

Personal Development:

The right to personal development of every law abiding individual has to be one of the most basic human rights of mankind. Restrictions to this right are experienced daily by the poor. Lack of access to education, to a decent living environment, to sufficient space for living and development - all these and a whole raft of other inhibiting factors to personal development have resulted in tens of thousands of Irish people never achieving anything remotely like their full potential as human beings throughout their lives. For those caught in the poverty trap, this inhumane situation continues from generation to generation in a never ending shameful cycle. While this scandalous blot on our nation waits to be redressed, thankfully, for the majority of citizens, the path to personal development is reasonably clear.

Planning and Personal Development:

While the role played by planning authorities in the past in the development of vast local authority housing estates including Ballymun and Moyross which exist as unemployment blackspots and areas of massive disadvantage is clear enough, the role of other aspects of the planning regime as they pertain to private housing and its relationship to personal development requires closer examination. To many who wish for the type of space for living available in the countryside, but who are forced instead by planning diktat to live in an urban area, this enforcement can impose serious restrictions on their right to personal development and achievement in a number of ways. These restrictions are further heightened by policies of high density urban housing. No matter what type of favourable spin planners and an Taisce attempt to ascribe to high density living, the fact remains that the more people you squeeze into one area, the smaller the space for living is available to each person. We have already made the point that there is universal acceptance of the direct relationship between the amount of personal space for living and the quality of life to be experienced.

Enforced high density living can directly restrict personal development in many ways. Psychologically, some people experience claustrophobic effects or suffer stress from the pressure of too many people constantly around them. Stress leads to ill health.

For many who work in offices, shops or factories all day or are unemployed, they need space at home or around their house to develop what may be for some simply hobby interests, or what may well be for others their true interests in life and the clear path to achieving their full potential. Examples of these activities are endless but could include carpentry, mechanical engineering, furniture restoring, painting, sculpture, music, making musical instruments, boat building, car maintenance, wood turning, candle making, D.I.Y. activities, gardening, birds and animals - the list goes on forever.

All these activities are part of normal human life throughout the world and throughout the ages. It is a monstrous proposition for city and town planners to say that the pursuit of virtually any of these interests is denied to citizens by virtue of their being forced to live in high density housing. The lack of space available either in or around these housing types can amount to an absolute ban on personal development.

Further downsides to lack of opportunities for development of latent interests or skills are frustration, loss of self confidence, stress, general unhappiness and or poor health. Children and teenagers also pay a price from high density living. Lack of space leads to enforced inactivity and boredom at a time in their lives when youthful activity is an essential component of good health.

Typical social problems involving teenagers in these situations are gangs, drinking, petty crime and drugs. These problems are not confined to any social class.

Aspirations:

Today's average family aspires to living in a house that complies with health and safety regulations and is fully serviced and insulated to a standard that offers an affordable good quality of life both within and around its confines. That is a reasonable aspiration.

Leaving aside the minority (and costly) interest in refurbishing old solid wall buildings to meet these aspirations, most families seeking a home have no choice but to either purchase a modern house or build a new one.

Towns and Street Villages:

Ireland's towns and street villages were either laid out to a landlords design or developed on an ad hoc basis over past historical periods - in any event, long before the car and other aspects of modern life came on the scene.

In general, town and village houses open directly on to the pavement. Back yards, sheds and lawns are mostly restricted in size due to the urban location.

All the older houses are of solid wall construction. Upgrading these houses to meet regulations and the aspirations of modern families (where it is possible) is expensive.

Many of these houses have the ground floor let for shops or offices. Families seeking space for living in these situations have to judge for themselves if town housing answers their requirements. The typical modern family with children will own a car or two, a buggy or pram, lots of clothes, children's and adults bikes, a child's swing, large toys, a dog and a cat, often a garage full of equipment and possessions associated with leisure activities or hobbies; a clothes line, perhaps a caravan, the list can go on and on.

Safety:
Safety issues in towns include car parking for the family car/s - where car space can be found - will it be outside the door or far removed from the house; safety for children from traffic passing the pavement all day; safety from air pollution created by traffic; safety and security from unlawful elements in the town; personal safety in some town areas at night; safety for children going to school; safety (and space) for children at play; safety from drugs.

Health:
Health issues in urban areas include air pollution, obesity in children from lack of exercise and the ready availability of junk food, stress caused by traffic congestion, stress caused to many vulnerable people by worries about personal security both within and outside the home; stress caused by children confined indoors or alternatively stress caused by worries over the safety of children playing outside the house.

Convenience:
Depending on the size of a town or village and where you live in it, many services such as shops, pubs, churches, hospitals, schools, welfare services etc may be easy to access. People must weigh up the advantages and disadvantages for themselves - if they are given a choice.
Under a planning regime enforcing urbanisation on the population such a choice will not be an option.

> Apart from old houses, many new housing estates are being built on the outskirts of villages and towns. Depending on cost, house type, location, density etc. people can make their own choices.

The Common Good

Chapter Four

Constitutional Rights:

If it is accepted that Irish people have the right to choose the communities in which they wish to live, then the planning issue is a simple matter of natural justice, i.e. people who wish to live in towns or villages have a right to do so and equally people who choose to live in the countryside also have a right to have their choice upheld. In either case, coercion by the state to force law abiding people to live in communities against their will is contrary to natural justice.

However, in all constitutional rights issues, the matter of the common good must be taken into account. The common good generally puts constraints of varying degrees on the rights of the individual and this is respected in a democracy.

Problems can arise however, in connection with the common good aspect as, for instance, in planning where disagreements on the interpretation of the common good sometimes end up in the courts. Thought the courts are there to protect the rights of both the individual and those of the common good, that line of action is rarely a reasonable option for individuals faced with planning refusals for houses in the open countryside—not least because of the formidable costs involved.

There is no level playing pitch in planning applications of this kind. All the weight of authority is on one side and if the state is intent on imposing a particular planning philosophy—albeit a UK philosophy—on the Irish people to force them to live in towns or street villages, they can coerce them into doing so by the not so subtle means of refusing them permission to build in the countryside.

By now, the Planners have assembled an almost impregnable armour of rules, regulations, conservational issues etc. to support the enforcement of its planning philosophy.

The following notes used by Professor Yvonne Scannall for a presentation on the Constitutional aspects of planning are published here to stimulate thinking and discussion on the topic.

Private Property Rights in the Constitution
Article 43

The State Acknowledges that man, in virtue of his rational being, has the natural right, antecedent to positive law, to the private ownership of external good.

The State may delimit by law the exercise of the said rights with a view to reconciling their exercise with the exigencies of the common good.

More Protection
Art 40.3 The State guarantees by its laws to respect and as far as practicable to defend and vindicate the personal rights of the citizen.

The State shall in particular, by its laws, protect as best it may from unjust attack and in the case of injustices done vindicate…the property rights of every citizen.

Consequently
Private property rights are very important in our democracy.
The basic human rights are life, liberty and property.

Magna Carta, Us Constitution, European Convention on Human Rights and Bunreacht.
Who decides what is for the common good?
Politicians, not Judges.
Planning is a restriction on property rights.
The Purpose of the Planning system: to balance and resolve competing demands between economic, social and environmental considerations to achieve sustainable development: An act to provide in the interests of the common good for proper planning and sustainable development…

What is sustainable development?
Sustainable development means the development that meets the needs of the present without compromising the ability of future generations to meet their own needs.

What is the common good?
A development plan is a plan indicating the development objectives for the area of the planning authority.

Central Dublin Development Association:

Development plans are only constitutional because made by elected members, people whose rights
may be affected have a chance to participate, they provide for the payment of compensation for those
whose rights are unduly restricted.

Objectives

Can relate to the sustainable development of the area:

Rural housing can be a matter of sustainable development: McGarry V Sligo CC

A Development Plan is a contract between the planning authority, developers and the public…

Planning in Practice.

Members of county councils can make the plans;

Sometimes irresponsible e.g. waste/travellers accommodation.

Powers removed and vested in the bureaucracy

Planning in Practice

Doesn't take account of social relatives/ Ballymore, Eustace or Tallaght.

Inconsistent policies

Developers contributions and benefits

Compensation.

Section 38 agreements

Ireland's Age of Building...
Urban

Ireland's Age of Building…
Rural

Democracy in Planning

Michael Healy Rae

It is my heartfelt belief that when planning permission is granted it should relate to whether or not it is sensible and practical to locate a house on a location and not go into the details of who is occupying the house. Basically a field or a piece of ground can take a house or not. Local authorities throughout Ireland have lost sight of this fact and in the process are depriving rural Ireland of many people who would be most welcome into it.

From a political point of view, looking after local people who were born in an area and ensuring that they can continue to live in land that might be made freely available to them through relatives, is of vital importance. The backbone of Irish communities has always been the continuation of local families living in the same area for generations. Complicated bureaucracy is hindering this. At a time when we are delighted that we have returning inward immigration, we should be doing everything possible to facilitate these people and while scenery has to be protected, people have lived in scenic locations for generations in our countryside. When the population of Ireland was many, many more times what it is at present they did not destroy the countryside they were living in but only enhanced it by the very culture and heritage that they had.

We can't be overrun and taken over by people with a flawed view on how our society should grow and develop and it is time to stand up and be counted at a national level because I honestly believe that local councillors throughout the country have their heart in the right place. Where is the legislation coming forward at national level to help improve the situation to allow development in the countryside? What we need to see at this stage is clear action and clear votes in the Dail in relation to changing the law and directing every local authority in the country to relax planning laws for rural applicants.

Propert Market
IAVI Report

Chapter Six

CONCLUSIONS & RECOMMENDATIONS

Conclusions

Sooner rather than later the Government must amend the Act and deal with matters which clearly:

- Undermine the traditional market forces that affect selling / supply / demand
- Prevent the establishment of any meaningful counter-flow, of those willing to live in rural areas, to the depopulation that has been underway for decades and that will be accelerated by the impending CAP Reform Proposals, due to be adopted in 2004.
- Create economic hardship for farmers
- Prevent many prospective home-owners from providing affordable housing for themselves
- Will embarrass Ireland in Europe, if successfully challenged by the European Commission
- Will embarrass central and local government in Ireland if successfully challenged in the courts.

Recommendations

Specifically, the IAVI recommends that Government should:

1 Examine the most recent census with a view to identifying depopulation blackspots.
2 Liaise with sporting bodies, the churches and the Department of Education to analyse the real impact, at local level, of underlying population-related trends.
3 Ensure the creation of a UNIFORM policy towards rural housing that reflects the diverse needs of different localities.
4 Ensure that planning conditions are fully enforced.
5 Prevent the widespread misuse of the planning process via groundless objections.
6 Question the role of An Taisce, in adopting such a vehemently negative stance in this area across the entire country.
7 Promote, through the planning process and regulations, wider use of bio cycling for drainage disposal, consequently enhancing sustainability by reducing

the use of septic tank drainage.

8   For one-off owner-occupied housing (regardless of the connectivity of the occupants to the locality) ensure that proper standards are imposed and enforced and that shared accesses are encouraged, while otherwise restricting development only on the following grounds:

    a) Adverse impact on a Special Amenity or Landscape Conservation Area

    b) Inadequate water provision, or foul drainage solution

    c) Serious traffic problems.

9   For holiday homes, ensure that they are erected in clusters, close to services and with approved group water and drainage schemes, in locations other than Special Amenity or Landscape Conservation Areas.

10   Extend and encourage the Rural Resettlement Schemes.

11   Extend the Rural Renewal Tax Designation provisions to the many areas not yet included.

12   Give priority to less-populated areas in the provision of one-off housing.

13   Examine the practical and academic background of planners operating in rural Ireland in order to ensure that planning is sympathetically controlled for local communities and is not, as at present, frequently divorced from the concerns and needs of such communities.

14   Encourage planners to meet and liaise with local communities to a much greater extent than at present.

15   Give consideration to the provision of grants and/or interest-free loans to private developers who are prepared to enhance the mains water, surface water, or foul sewerage disposal systems in villages. A developer, who might build an additional say 20-30 houses in a village, would undertake the work involved, but the improved infrastructure would benefit the existing population, while leaving open the possibility of additional houses being provided in the future. Such a provision, where there was an evident and immediate benefit to the local community from a new housing development, might well help curtail some of the groundless objections to planning applications.

See Appendix for Full Report

Urban Areas
Critical Mass Theory

Chapter Seven

National Population Imbalance
Urban: Population increasing all the time. (See Appendix—Housing and Democracy)

Urban living - costs to the nation
Irish taxpayers (including rural taxpayers) pay the cost of providing the basic infrastructure for towns and cities. This includes streets, bridges, ring roads, motorways, public transport, street lighting, sewage pipes and treatment plants, water supply and reservoirs. The taxpayer also subsides services such as water, waste collection, public transport, gas, energy, street cleaning, maintenance of public buildings, parks, traffic control, parking, art, theatre, museums, concert halls etc.

Pollution:

High density urban living produces high levels of pollution of many kinds; traffic pollution, noise pollution, air pollution, water pollution, domestic waste, industrial pollution, pollution of rivers and the sea. Massive amounts of urban generated waste are dumped in land fill sites in rural areas. All pollution lowers the quality of life.

Critical Mass:

The theory of a definable critical mass of people concentrated in any one town or city as being essential for the provision of services is so nebulous as to be meaningless. Every argument put forward in favour is counterbalanced by an equal argument against.

For example, cities can be (and are) anything from perhaps 20,000 to 40 million people and all numbers in between. Where in there is the perfect critical mass? Also, cities continuously grow and expand—that is their nature. Does the critical mass aspect also continually change?

Is there an ideal critical mass to be aspired to for the provision of services in all situations? If so, what are these essential services - should each city have an airport, a metro, a university, major hospitals, prisons, drug centres, an opera house, sports stadium etc etc. Where is the line drawn? Who decides?
The continual expansion of cities sucks in people from rural areas. In many cases this contributes to total depopulation. Evidence of this phenomenon is to be seen all over the developed world.
Ireland is going the same way.

This pursuit of a mythical critical mass for urban living, which can result in rural deserts, is certainly not in the national interest.
* The argument is continuously put forward that rural living is subsidised by urban dwellers and that this burden is unsustainable.

The facts tell a different story.

Rural Living - costs to the nation?

Roads:

About one third of the population live in dispersed villages. The road network that serves these scattered communities has developed over thousands of years. Like many other public services these eventually become the responsibility of local authorities and have been upgraded and maintained to standards appropriate to modern life. They are mainly secondary and minor roads.

Ireland's Age of Building…
Infrastructure

Present planning policies of refusals in open countryside, taken together with other factors including the decline in farming is leading to serious rural depopulation. Fewer, or in many cases, no households at all being served by many country roads will inevitably result in local authorities refusing to maintain them. In turn this will quickly lead to dereliction, overgrown roads, impassable roads, clogged water courses, potholed roads, - in short, an environmental disaster.

All citizens are entitled to be served by public roads (where possible). Common logic indicates that the greater the number of country houses served by public roads, the greater value for money to the state from its investment in maintenance. The national cost of upgrading and maintaining this road network, which serves one third of the population (new roads are hardly ever provided) bears no realistic comparison to the massive costs of providing new roads, motorways, flyovers, bridges, dual carriageways, tunnels, by-passes, roundabouts, city trams, traffic control systems etc. which serve the other two thirds of the population who live in the cities and towns.

Modern life is marked by a highly mobile population. In practice this means that urban dwellers spend some time driving on rural roads in the same way as rural dwellers spend some time driving in our cities and towns. Everyone benefits from a good national road network.

Electricity:

In view of the traditional dispersed village pattern of rural housing, the Irish government introduced the Rural Electrification Scheme in 1947. As a result of this enlightened policy, electricity has been available in virtually all rural areas for over fifty years. As with the road network, the more users there are in any area, the cheaper the cost of providing and maintaining the service. The cost of providing

electricity to rural areas cannot be reasonably looked at as a stand-alone cost which is separate from providing electricity to towns and cities.

By and large, electricity is generated in rural areas e.g. Moneypoint / Tarbert, and delivered to all parts of the country via the national network of pylons and poles. Cities and towns couldn't be supplied without this network. Nowadays, the network is also used to convey electricity which is being generated by wind farms in remote areas. This is destined to become more important in the future.

"Real costs:"

If we extend the argument of charging the so called `real costs' of providing services to citizens, no matter where they live, such as more expensive postage stamps to rural areas, then the converse is equally true and people living close to generating stations should be charged less for electricity than people living hundreds of miles away.

Connection Costs: A standard charge of E1, 338 applies to all new connections made in rural areas (within 500 yards of a line). This cost is borne by the house owner and represents no cost to the taxpayer. Rural customers already pay higher line rental charges than city users.

We are also told that the costs of making main roads through rural areas is higher than equivalent roads in cities because of land costs, but as the main users of these trunk roads are city and town dwellers who cris cross the country on their legitimate business, here again, the `real cost' argument becomes meaningless.

Water:

Group Water Schemes bring piped water to rural communities all over the country. Though grant aided, essential core funding comes from the financial contributions of all home owners connected to the scheme.

Summary:

All services for rural living are already in place except sewage treatment. This aspect is paid for by each home owner (septic tank) and represents no cost to the nation.

Rural Depopulation

Chapter Eight

Depopulation:
Results:

Isolation of families and elderly, run down of essential services such as primary schools, small shops, post offices, doctors, banks, buses, pastoral care, youth activities, rise in rural unemployment etc.

Social life suffers in all aspects e.g. sports, churches, local events, festivals, cultural activities, pubs, restaurants, tourism related activities, breakdown of traditional community life.

These losses contribute directly to a general lowering of community morale, a loss of confidence in the future, serious loss of identity and further out migration from rural areas.

Rural communities are often the direct conduit through which much of our rich cultural heritage, including our language, is transmitted from previous generations.

The failure of this conduit due to depopulation, not alone affects local folklore, culture and traditions but as each rural area represents an intrinsic part of the greater patchwork of our national cultural heritage, then the entirety suffers irreparable damage.

Planning for the Survival of Rural Areas.

Dr. Jerry Cowley.

As one who had lived almost all of my life in urban areas, it was a revelation to come to live in a rural area of County Mayo. What struck most of all was the closeness which existed between people compared to the urban situation, where you might hardly know your neighbour except to pass greetings to each other on the street. As Chairman of the Rural Doctor's Group, I was well aware through the commissioning of original research of the continuing depopulation of Irish Rural practice populations. Areas where the population would drop to a critical level meant that a particular area would lose their GP. It struck me that this continuing depopulation was leading to the demise of rural areas. An entire rural culture was fast disappearing before our eyes. I first described and highlighted the "vicious circle" of loss of services from rural areas with continuing depopulation. I flagged the migration of rural populations to the larger urban centres. After all, who could be expected to live in an area where there are no basic services remaining such as the local doctor in illness; where there is no Garda to provide protection from marauding criminals; no school for the education of children or no post offices to send a letter? What was needed to break this vicious circle was to provide the basic infrastructure, which could hold people in an area. It struck me that communities were haemorrhaging their population from both ends - we were losing our young people through lack of employment opportunity and also our older people through the sad silent migration of older people to faraway institutions. The St. Brendan's Village concept supports older people by giving them the opportunity to stay locally, no matter how old or disabled they are. This has not only stopped, but actually reversed the sad, silent migration of older people to faraway institutions. St. Brendan's Village is now recognised as an EU model of best practice of supporting older people in their own community. It is also the biggest local employer.

The "Safe Home" programme has secured permanent accommodation all over Ireland for over 240 long-term older Irish emigrants. Rural Resettlement Ireland has done similar work for families from large urban areas.

All of the above depends heavily on the provision of housing in rural areas. Rural housing is the most basic of all essential infrastructure. If we are to retain the rural ethos then we need to retain our people, young and old, in rural areas. This can only happen if people, young and old, have a place to stay and this means rural housing. So much depends on official policy. If the policy, as laid down in County Development Plans does not allow people to build and settle in rural areas, then we are all doomed to eventually form part of the urban jungle, which is no substitute for our rich rural way of life. Whatever policy is enacted on rural planning, it is only as good as its implementation, and this must be ensured through proper legislation.

Future of Farming

Future of farming / community life

In its Statement of Strategy 2003-2005 the Department of Agriculture and Food says:
"Recent decades have seen significant change in farming. While farm numbers are declining distinct categories of farmers are emerging as full time farmers, part-time farmers and transitional farmers. The Government's commitment ......is to maintaining the greatest number of family farms through the development of a core of full time farmers, while at the same time ensuring that other farm households have the opportunity to supplement their income through off-farm employment by means of a combination of on land and off farm enterprises. Part time farming will continue to offer many farm families, who wish to remain on the land, and opportunity to maintain living standards in line with the norm in our society".

The ongoing decline in farm numbers officially acknowledged in the above statement is also true of other developed countries. While official policy in Ireland is to try and keep people on the land through part time farming etc., serious depopulation in many areas is an unavoidable consequence of this decline.

Rural community life, like urban life, requires essential services. Schools, shops, post offices, doctors, Gardai, transport, professional and many other services need sufficient people in order to keep going. Non farmers who live in rural areas also have to be able to earn a living. Some categories of self employed like artists, craft workers, writers, some computer workers, builders, alternative medicine practitioners, vets, small light industries etc., can operate from home. The majority however, need to travel to work. This latter category of rural commuters is castigated by the opponents of rural housing and faces a particularly hard, if not impossible, task in obtaining planning. Their positive contribution to community life is ignored and they are regarded exclusively in a negative light.

However, car ownership and commuting is a universal phenomenon in modern life whether one lives in an urban or a rural environment. (See appendix).

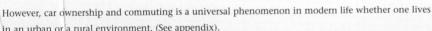

Chapter Nine

The effects of rural depopulation

In singling out rural commuters for special condemnation on spurious environmental grounds, planners and their supporters in the anti-rural housing brigade, expose the one dimensional, culturally impoverished core of a forced urbanisation policy.

It must be pointed out again and again that it is not just Government Policy but also the plainest of common sense, that if the inevitable change in the rural population from predominantly farmers to predominantly non farmers is not allowed to take place in a natural and organic way, our once thriving communities will wither and die simply from lack of numbers.

The bottom line is that there will never be sufficient numbers of people involved in agriculture again to sustain services and vibrant rural communities without a majority of non farmers living in the countryside.

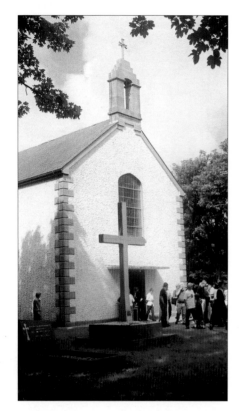

Rural Communities - a case for special conservation

The IRDAs stated aspiration of striving to ensure the growth and maintenance of a vibrant populated countryside into the future, with particular reference to the traditional Irish form of the baile fearann or dispersed village, is in complete harmony with government policy.

The following extracts taken from the White Paper on Rural Development (1999) refer to Government commitments on the matter. The last extract is taken from a speech delivered by an Taoiseach Bertie Ahern in Maam Cross in 2003.

White Paper: Government Commitments

"...to maintain vibrant rural communities in rural areas and to establish a comprehensive policy response for that purpose"

"Individuals and families will have a real choice as to whether to stay in, leave or move to rural Ireland".

"Rural" - spatial units consisting of small towns and villages with populations of 1,500 or 3,000 inhabitants respectively and their hinterlands"

"All Government policies and interventions which are directed towards improving the physical, economic and social conditions of people living in the open countryside, in coastal areas, tows and villages..."

"Rural development and the well being of the rural community is a public good. The economic, social and cultural development of rural areas should not be passively dictated to by market forces alone". "To achieve the aim of a balanced rural population, planning policy should, as far as possible, facilitate people willing to settle in rural areas...".

"Settlement pattern....Sustaining dispersed rural communities in towns, villages and the countryside in their hinterlands".

Policy Advisory Group June 1997
"Local Authority Housing programmes should encourage and support public housing development... including the countryside, villages and small towns. Rural communities should be encouraged to exploit the possibilities which rural resettlement programmes provide for the regeneration of their areas. These actions would help to revitalise the rural population and underpin service provision in mainly rural areas"

Extract from An Taoiseach's speech.
"In publishing the National Spatial Strategy, we have sent a clear signal that the traditional settlement pattern of rural Ireland is something that we value and should be developed. I recognise that the countryside of the dispersed village or townland or `baile fearann' as it is called in Irish, is as real a village to those that live in it as town or city is to urban dwellers. The traditional loyalties to townland parish and county have been a binding force in Ireland over that last 100 years and have been a major motivational force in social and economic development".

In the same speech he said *"The growth of our towns and cities, which is very welcome, should not be at the expense of rural areas".*

The difficulty is that there is no evidence to suggest that planning authorities around the country either take heed of or actively implement policies favourable towards the dispersed village. On the contrary, the reason why the IRDA was founded in the first place was the recognition that a united front is needed to combat planning policies being imposed in rural areas which have the direct opposite effect and which will hasten the end of the dispersed community so lovingly referred to by an Taoiseach.

In implementing these policies, issues surrounding landscape quality, waste water treatment, road safety, heritage, environment, endangered species, wild life, special areas of conservation and a whole raft of rules and regulations governing occupancy, sterilization of land etc. are used liberally to refuse permission for houses in the open countryside. The policy to refuse is matched by a policy designed instead to force people into high density housing in towns and villages.

Or so it seems to the average rural—or would be—rural dweller. Individuals are at a complete loss to understand how the state and its leader, an Taoiseach Bertie Ahern, can express such concern for the dispersed village—a concern which is seemingly echoed by elected county councillors throughout the land—while in reality, a contrary planning philosophy, emanating clearly from our UK dominated professional planning regime, is the policy being enforced.

The dilemma must be faced fairly and squarely by the government and corrective action taken on behalf of the people.

As a first and immediate step, the government must declare the survival of dispersed villages a conservation issue and the people—homo sapiens—who inhabit them an endangered species. This proposal is a logical extension of both EU and national Government policies of issuing protection orders for various species of animals, birds and other sections of our ecology which are perceived to be under threat. The IRDA regard the human species which has inhabited the rural countryside for thousands of years, as being, at the very least, as worthy of government protection as the ecological examples mentioned above.

The reasons for the alarming population drop in rural areas are complex; they relate to farming and other issues and are well documented. These same issues, or variants of them, occur in other developed countries, often resulting in the entire desertification of huge areas of countryside where normal human life no longer exists. It is difficult to imagine that such a scenario could happen in Ireland but unfortunately serious and often terminal depopulation has already occurred in many areas of the Midlands and the West. With the numbers involved in farming in continuing decline, further depopulation is inevitable.

If, as already stated, the first step to save the situation, is a government directive to preserve traditional dispersed village communities, then the next step is to put in place measures to support that directive.

Support Measures:

Planning authorities would be required to proof all applications for houses in the open countryside against the directive. To ensure that this was done in a fair and open manner, the IRDA must be given a statutory role in the planning process, similar to that of An Taisce. Local depopulation, falling school numbers and other vital factors would be taken into account on a case by case basis.

National Conservation Plan: Ordinance Survey Maps.

A study of the Ordinance Survey maps over the past 160 Years would show clearly where farm houses existed in the past. These houses, scattered throughout the countryside formed the basis of the dispersed villages.

This concrete evidence of rural community life should now form the basis for a national preservation plan.

As a rule of thumb, planning should be given in any place where a house existed in the past. For site specific reasons this might not be possible in all cases but at least the overall ethos would be that of a positive approach to the rebuilding of rural communities as opposed to the presumption of refusal which applies to rural planning applications today. New greenfield sites would also get full and fair assessment.

Farming / rural communities: All notions currently in vogue in our planning regime that rural planning be confined to people connected with the land (i.e. farming or agri- business) will have to change completely. The stark reality is that less than 8% of the population is now involved with agriculture. This trend is worldwide (in developed countries) and is going in a downward direction all the time.

The over riding consideration in the survival of scattered rural communities has to be the numbers of people who live there. Traditionally the majority of these people would have been involved in farming while the minority would have had other occupations such as carpenters, weavers, shoemakers, fishermen, builders, teachers, musicians and so on. Taken together, they formed a homogenous culturally rich and diverse community.

But now that the whole picture has changed - not alone in Ireland but around the developed world - and the proportion of farmers to other types of occupations is reversed, it is quite irrational to ban people in other occupations from building houses if community numbers are to be kept up.

That is of course, if there is a genuine concern at government level for rural community life and if there isn't, in fact, quite a different agenda at work, i.e. an attempt to depopulate rural areas except for a few ranch type farmers and to herd the rest of the population into high density life styles in towns and villages.

Sustainability
Cathal MacGabhann

The most frequent argument in favour of the compulsory urbanisation of the country and the desertification of rural Ireland in the future is that rural settlement is environmentally unsustainable.

Six issues relating to sustainability have been raised in the debate about rural housing

(1) Increased construction costs

(2) Increased public maintenance costs

(3) Increased emissions of CO_2 through increased use of cars

(4) Depletion of finite land areas

(5) Consequent depletion of agricultural output.

(6) Depletion of natural habitat through loss of natural hedgerows.

Increased Construction Costs:

The economics of scale certainly apply to the construction of houses. However, in Ireland today, the total cost of a rural home on a half acre site is less than the cost of a similar house on a one 10th acre site in an urban housing estate. The reasons for this are the following:

(a) The existing urban planning regime has resulted in increasing pressure on the cost of suitable housing land in urban locations and has (unwittingly) assisted developers in increasing site costs of urban housing with the result that site costs now account for 50% of the total costs of houses in Dublin and other large urban centres. In the case of rural housing the site costs are in the region of 10 - 15% of total cost.

(b) In urban housing the cost of new roads and footpaths, public lighting, trafficlights, new schools and playing fields, public sewage and waste water disposal have to be taken into account, whether included in the cost to the purchaser or paid for by the State. In the case of rural housing no new infrastructure is required at public expense. The existing road network, group water schemes, rural electricity network etc is used together with existing schools, playing fields etc. The home owners pay for the connection to utilities and for their own waste treatment plants. Footpaths, public lighting, traffic lights etc are not required. Additional rural housing makes the existing infrastructure more economical. These networks would still be required to service the diminishing agricultural community even if there was no new rural housing.

(c) Rural housing gives employment to thousands of provincial architects, engineers, builders, tradesmen, construction workers etc. who have lower overheads than large urban companies and operate in lower profit margins. These in turn and rural dwellers in general, contribute to the viability of hundreds of towns and villages throughout a country which would otherwise decline with the reduction in numbers working in agriculture.

Maintenance Costs:

The existing rural infrastructure network must be maintained even as the numbers wholly employed in agriculture declines from the present 100,000 to 30,000 to 20,000 in 25 years time as forecast. There will also be a considerable number of part time farmers who will travel to work in surrounding towns and cities, commuting an average 15 miles to work. This essential infrastructure will become increasingly uneconomic unless there is a substantial increase in the number of rural dwellers not employed in agriculture. The road network, for example, will be an essential part of a future tourist industry. Similarly a minimum number of rural schools will be necessary in any event.

Accordingly rural housing will make the national infrastructure more economical and will make provincial villages more viable without any additional marginal cost.

Emissions:

There are no public transport systems in provincial Ireland in the real sense of the word. Two or three busses per day plus school busses don't constitute a Transport System. Thankfully, car-ownership is now enjoyed by nearly all families, and rural people help each other out with lifts etc. (insurance notwithstanding) There is only a real public transport system in Dublin and in one or two other large centres, yet in Dublin where there are over 600,000 private cars and an excellent public transport system 59% of workers travel to work in private cars which now travel at 5-8 miles per hour in the city. Emissions depend to a great extent on fuel consumption and a car travelling 15 miles to work in a provincial town at 50/60 miles per hour produces less emissions than one in Dublin travelling at 5-8 miles per hour. In addition rural dwellers usually surround their homes with hedges, ornamental shrubs and trees which contribute to reducing the effects of emissions.

Depletion of Finite Land Area:

As a result of our tragic history, Ireland suffered the unique experience in Europe of a decline in population from 8,500,000 in 1845 to about 50% of that in 1971. Since then the population has increased somewhat but is not much more than 60% of the 1845 level and at present we have the lowest population density in the E.U. south of the Arctic Circle - 54 per sq.km as compared with 390 in England, 388 in the Netherlands, 336 in Belgium, 230 in Germany etc.

If we were to build 10,000 rural homes on 1/2 acre sites for the next 20 years the total of 200,000 houses would occupy 100,000 acres or 0.57% of our land area.

If sites on marginal land were preferred there would be no loss of agricultural potential and many thousands of marginal farmers would benefit instead of a relatively small number of extremely wealthy developers. This would help them to stay in agriculture, help family members to build homes locally or obtain third level education and would be a wholly positive use of resources, socially and economically.

Depletion of Agricultural Output:

As already explained, the percentage of agricultural land which would be taken up by the construction of more rural homes would be infinitesimal. The farmers, selling sites, would favour disposal of poor land and any potential loss of agricultural output would be minimal. The common agricultural policy is increasingly focused on reduction of output and letting the market influence production and on assisting third world countries to take a greater share of world food production.

Depletion of Natural Habitat through Loss of Natural Hedgerows:

This point could only be made by people with no knowledge of rural living. In point of fact, each new rural home results in a new half acre field with up to an additional 200 yards of hedge. Each rural holding also results in the growth of many hedges, shrubs, trees, vegetables, gardens etc. all which improve the habitat for wildlife. Rural dwellers are normally animal lovers who enjoy a flourishing natural environment and treasure the landscape in which they live.

City Traffic.
Average distance travelled in an hour, 5–8 miles…

Rural Traffic.
…Average distance travelled in an hour, 50 miles.

The Myth of extraordinary car dependency in Ireland

Dr. Seamus Caulfield. 12/04/04

Over the last year, at numerous conferences, in submissions to Government and in articles and letters to the newspapers and other statements to the media, reference has been made to this State's extraordinary car dependency. It is claimed that we drive our cars at twice the European average of total kilometres per annum, the highest in the world and even 30% higher than the USA. The source of this information comes from James Nix, the vice chairman of An Taisce and a researcher in Transport and Land-Use studies. His source is a book, Transport Investment and Economic Development, published in 2000, which takes its information from British Transport statistics from 1997 which in turn take their information from European Statistics and estimates from the early 1990's.

The data presented refer to vehicle kilometres per annum which is very different to passenger kilometres per annum. Why a researcher in Transport Studies would chose to cite fossil fourth/fifth hand "statistics" while ignoring contemporary first hands sources such as those emanating from Eurostat, the European Environment Agency and DG7 is difficult to understand. The European Environment Agency in its TERM 2002, 12 EU fact sheets points out that for vehicle kilometres "only very limited and low-quality data is available" and in a footnote lists the seven of the 15 member states for which data are available. Ireland is not included among the seven.

Contemporary first hand statistics from the European sources listed above indicate that Ireland has one of the best if not the overall best record in Europe in achieving some of the EU transport objectives. Despite the fact that we have had extraordinary GDP growth during the 1990's, we have succeeded in achieving decoupling between GDP growth and "motorisation" (cars per thousand of population) growth, a de-coupling not achieved by the EU. Our passenger kilometres per annum based on estimates and statistics from DG7 is one of the lowest in the EU. We have the second lowest expenditure on transport as a percentage of GDP. In freight transport, Ireland has had even more spectacular success in achieving decoupling between tonne-kilometre growth and GDP growth (TERM 2002 13 EU). Ireland has had the lowest rate in the EU in 1991 and while five other countries showed some progress in 1999, none has yet achieved the Irish 1991 level while Ireland has succeeded in reducing still further its tonne kilometre per unit of GDP by a third in the eight years. The Irish figure had reduced from over 60% of the EU average in 1991 to approximately 35% in 1999. A more recent study of Irish vehicle kilometres in 2002 may alter somewhat our very high positive ranking in the EU when comparative statistics from other countries are available but our still low level of motorisation compared to the EU average is unlikely to change the overall positive ranking of this, the most rural country in the EU.

Holiday Homes

Holiday Homes are a worldwide phenomenon. They have been around for a long time and are more directly linked to affluence than to any political ideology. They have ranged in scale from castles in the countryside owned by urban members of the aristocracy to tiny fishing huts owned by more humble urban dwellers.

Whether people who can afford to, choose to buy or build their holiday homes in their own country or in some other country, the underlying reasons are the same .i.e. the locations in each case represent the personal choice of where the owner wishes to spend some holiday time. There may be secondary reasons relating to property investment, shared ownership, family reasons etc. High on the list of attractions for choice of location are coastal areas, beaches, lakes, mountains and weather. Local culture, traditions, food, drink and customs also play a part. The same attractions also give rise to the growth of the mainstream tourist industry in these areas worldwide. Increasing affluence results in increased housing and construction of all kinds in the worlds' most renowned tourist resorts.

In Ireland the tourist industry is a major part of the national economy and the spend from visitors renting holiday homes amounts to hundreds of millions of Euro annually (see Bord Fáilte figures below).

In reality, there is absolutely no turning back the tide of the holiday home phenomenon. It is here to stay and is far more likely to increase rather than decrease in scale.

However, there are mixed feelings and quite opposite views expressed on the issue of holiday homes.
- To those who can afford them the main issue is the extra dimension that owning a holiday home can bring to the quality of their lives.

They can also be useful revenue earners for their owners when rented to other visitors—especially where tax incentive schemes apply.

- To local people who may be refused planning permission for permanent homes, the vista of large numbers of holiday homes standing empty for most of the year represents a basic injustice in the planning system which threatens the survival of many depopulated coastal and rural communities.

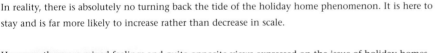

Chapter Twelve

- To small farmers struggling at subsistence level on poor land in coastal areas where for generations the only hope for their children was emigration, opportunities to sell sites for holiday homes can mean education and advancement for their families at home in Ireland rather than in Boston or elsewhere in the world.

- Or the chance to sell a small portion of their land in sites can allow small farmers to invest in improving their farming activities in ways that may underpin their future viability. The sale of sites also means that these small farmers who are at the heart of rural communities, can at long last reap some personal benefit in the quality of their own lives from a tourist industry that for centuries has exploited their natural friendliness, traditions and culture to line everybody else's pockets, while they themselves remained amongst the poorest people in the country.

- To pubs, restaurants, hotels, gift shops and other commercial enterprises providing services for the tourist industry, people either owning or renting holiday homes form a clearly quantifiable section of their customer base.

Overseas visitors renting holiday cottages or similar accommodation may spend more per day on services than the owners of holiday homes down for the weekend bringing their own groceries with them, but that said, every single occupier of holiday accommodation is there as a visitor and therefore makes a contribution to the overall local economy—even if it doesn't go beyond ice cream for the children and a few drinks for the parents.

Value / Contribution of Holiday Homes to Tourism.
Estimate of the value/contribution of both overseas visitors and domestic tourists staying in both rented accommodation (individual and group schemes) and holiday homes. The estimate is based on the broad assumption that an overseas visitor or domestic tourist spends the same on a per diem basis irrespective of where he/she stays (clearly you would expect someone staying in a holiday home with no payment involved to spend less than someone staying in paid accommodation), so the estimates should be used with caution.

Also, the overseas visitors estimates are based on all visitors irrespective of the purpose of visit and include students/contract workers who spend a long time in rented accommodation. The number of nights rented accommodation by holiday visitors, particularly in respect of M Europe and other areas, would be a lot lower, however, all visitors, whatever their reason for visit, will contribute to the local economies.

Rented Accommodation and Holiday Homes

2002	Britain	M. Europe	N. America	Other	Total
Overseas Visitors (000s)	3,452	1,378	844	245	5,919
% using Rented Acc	7	12	5	10	8
No. using Rented Acc (000s)	233	159	45	24	461
% using Holiday Homes	2	1	2	1	2
No. using Holiday Homes (000s)	78	13	13	4	108
Overseas Visitor Nights (000s)	18,290	15,358	8,053	3,644	45,346
% in Rented Acc	13	30	11	31	20
Nights in Rented Acc (000s)	2,433	4,637	891	1,124	9,095
% in Holiday Homes	3	1	4	1	2

2002	Britain	M Europe	N America	Other	Total
Nights in Holiday Homes (000s)	564	159	344	50	1,117
Total Nights in Rented and Holiday Homes	3,007	4,796	1,235	1,174	10,212
Average per diam spend (€)	70.16	56.43	88.04	62.76	
Expenditure Estimate (€ million)	211.0	270.6	108.7	73.7	664.0

Domestic Tourism

	Ireland
Domestic Nights in Rented (000s)	1,550
Domestic Nights in Own Holiday Homes (000s)	1,135
Total Nights in Rented and Holiday Home (000s)	2,685
Average Domestic per diem Spend (€)	55.75
Domestic Expenditure (€ million)	149.7

Tourism / Landscape

Chapter Thirteen

Tourism

There are many misconceptions about the attractiveness of our countryside vis-a-vis the numbers of families living in it.

Local authorities make a big issue of this aspect and many refusals result from restrictive policies interpreted through the subjective opinions of planners as to siting of houses in so called visually vulnerable areas. These misconceptions must be examined and challenged. Also the claim of the importance of tourism to the local economy of individual areas must be examined and weighed against the detrimental affect of depopulation caused in large part by planning refusals.

The whole question of houses in traditional dispersed villages and their affect on tourism is widely used to deny natural justice to citizens and rob them of their constitutional rights. However, a study of relevant tourist facts tells a different story.

Example: (a)

Gweedore, the Gaeltacht area in north west Donegal, is a thickly populated rural district with houses everywhere as far as the eye can see. They are perched on outcrops of rocky landscape where ever a site for a house could be found as well as on the flat.

They face in all directions. This is the traditional way housing has developed over many generations. Twenty five thousand people live in Gweedore. The area is recognised as the most densely populated non-urban area of its kind in Europe.

By modern standards, however, a planners worst nightmare.

If we were to apply the planners' theory that houses destroy the landscape and deter tourists, then the Gweedore district should be the biggest tourist turn-off in Europe. The reality however, is quite the opposite. Tourism plays a major role in the local economy; Gweedore is one of the premier tourist attractions in Co. Donegal. There is no record of complaints from tourists pointing to the numbers of houses in the area.

Elsewhere in Ireland, similar anomalies occur.

Example (b):

The Loop Head peninsula in Clare is the most sparsely populated area in the county and is suffering continual decline since the famine (60% decline since 1926)

In spite of its spectacular natural beauty it attracts only a tiny fraction of the tourists who visit the county. Tour busses which visit Bunratty Castle, Ennis and other heavily populated areas in large numbers are never seen on the West Clare peninsula. Apart from Irish people who own holiday homes in Kilkee and other sea side villages, overseas tourism plays a very minor role in the general economy of Loop Head. B&B's as well as pubs and restaurants have a very short tourist season and employment in the industry is small and mostly part time.

Tourism: Bord Fáilte Figures

General information (average numbers 1997–2001)

Approximately 6 million overseas tourists visit Ireland annually.

(a) Regional examples: 3.3 million go to the Dublin region—the most densely populated part of Ireland.

(b) The West region (Galway, Mayo, Roscommon)

Total overseas tourists	**1,149,000**	
Breakdown by county:		
Galway	939,000	(60% of revenue spent in Galway city)
Mayo	296,000	
Roscommon	51,000	

These figures in (a) and (b) clearly show that the majority of tourists are attracted to visit the most densely populated regions of Dublin and Galway by comparison with the smaller numbers who visit Mayo and Roscommon. Both of these latter counties are very rural.

Example: Midlands East region (excluding Dublin)

Overseas visitors 2001	
Kildare	150,000
Laois	37,000
Longford	32,000
Louth	89,000
Meath	90,000
Wicklow	262,000
Offaly East	40,000
Westmeath	126,000

From the above figures, it is clear that the most densely populated areas, i.e. Kildare, Louth, Meath, Wicklow and West Meath attract the greatest numbers of tourists.

Laois, Longford and Offaly East, all very rural areas, attract by far the smallest numbers of tourists.

Taking the country as a whole, counties Cavan, Leitrim, Monaghan, Tipperary North, Offaly West, Carlow, Laois, Longford, Offaly East—all very rural areas—attract only a small fraction of the total numbers of tourists who visit Ireland.

The majority go to the most densely populated counties.

The argument put forward by planners and an Taisce that tourists mainly come to see the green fields of Ireland don't stand up when assessed against Bord Fáilte statistics.

"Results since the year 2000 show that overseas visitor spending in the West has remained static compared to Dublin where visitor spending is up over 30% during the same period. Given these figures, it is crucial to address the East / West imbalance in tourism. While the dispersion of tourist throughout the Region gets prominence in the National Development Plan, unfortunately, the opposite is happening on the ground".
Brian Flynn, Chief Executive of Ireland West Tourism

"Overseas visitors choose to visit Ireland mainly because of its rural attractions and not because of its cities", the chairman, the chairman of Fáilte Ireland, Ms Gillian Bowler said.

"Yet despite Ireland's rural attractiveness, and a growth in numbers, overseas visitors were by and large not travelling outside urban areas. Three in four bed nights outside of Dublin were accounted for by Irish customers last year. There needed to be a greater regional spread", she said.
Irish Times 04 March 2004

Where people live in a country has the most profound significance for the cultural, social and economic life of its inhabitants. In Ireland, settlement patterns which have emerged and developed over thousands of years have become inextricably woven into this cultural fabric. Attempts by bureaucrats, planners or even governments to make changes as fundamental as the enforced urbanisation of the rural population as though it were all a numbers game, will, if they succeed, have the most catastrophic effects on Irish life.

Making use of the visual appearance of the landscape as almost the sole reason for justifying the dismissal of an entire national culture is so one dimensional, so shallow and so lacking in any depth of thought - philosophic, humane or otherwise - that this approach must be exposed for the destructive force that it is.

This approach could be likened to looking at a cardboard cut out of a person and saying that this one dimensional image gave a complete and rounded picture of all aspects of that person, their personality, their feelings and their entire life story.

Whatever the merits of a cardboard image, we know that to make all these other claims would be nonsense.

Water Quality

There is a rightful and universal concern about water pollution from all sewage treatment systems. The overall aspiration is the same, ie. to eliminate water pollution by all sewage treatment plants.

Chapter Fourteen

"Drinking water is now synonymous with treated water.... All public water supplies as well as group water schemes... are required by law to meet...Drinking Water Regulation...standards"

Department of Environment, Heritage and Local Government.

EPA Report 2004
Only 8% of urban waste
water is fully treated

23% of urban waste
water did not receive
any treatment

Water / Waste Water (EPA Reports)

The Environmental Protection Agency published three reports in February 2004 dealing with water quality, phosphorous regulations and waste water discharges. In general as would be expected the reports indicated improvements in most areas and overall a not unsatisfactory level. In a country with a mild climate, a low population density and an adequate annual rainfall, this situation would be considered normal. However, in some areas there were negative reports.

For example, there is complete treatment of urban waste water in only 8% of cases. 23% of waste water arising did not receive any form of treatment. The situation is improving but at very considerable expense. National estimates are not available but to correct the situation in County Kerry alone would cost €115 million.

With regard to the quality of drinking water, public water supplies are provided for 91.9% of the population. Overall, compliance with standards in public water supplies amounted to 97.4%. For the 8.1% of group water schemes the overall compliance rate was 91.5%.

For rural homes the waste treatment system recommended by the EPA consists of septic tanks. However many of the septic tanks in the country were installed 30 or 40 years ago when current standards did not apply. These might now be inspected and installations which are not efficient might be brought up to standard with suitable grant assistance at a fraction of the cost of establishing a proper standard of treatment of urban waste water discharges at public expense.

With regard to Phosphorous regulations the report indicates that 61.8% of monitoring stations are compliant with the regulations. This would appear to be unsatisfactory but there are many factors affecting the water quality in this respect.

Overall it is clear that rural housing does not contribute to any significant degree of deterioration in water quality or contamination of the environment either directly or indirectly.

Appendix Septic tank systems

Septic Tanks Sewage:
The cost of providing the infrastructure for sewage treatment in cities and towns is paid for by the taxpayers. Taxes are collected in both urban and rural areas and the national exchequer does not distinguish between these two sources when distributing funds to Local Authorities. Therefore, taxpayers who live in rural areas also pay for urban sewage treatment plants from which they derive no benefit.

Septic tanks:
In contrast to urban dwellers that pay no direct charges for sewage treatment, rural dwellers pay the full cost of both installing and maintaining their own septic tanks. Planning authorities insist on an annual service contract being in place for each new house. This represents a substantial annual cost to rural dwellers which doesn't exist for city dwellers.

Water Quality:
There is a rightful and universal concern about water pollution from all sewage treatment systems. Many urban systems are antiquated and inadequate - some pump untreated sewage into lakes, rivers and the sea. It is estimated that the cost of upgrading urban systems to meet E.U. standards will be 3 billion Euro. Some of this work is underway with both urban and rural taxpayers the costs.

Whereas, in many cases, urban dwellers have had the benefit of toilets and running water since the 19th Century, rural dwellers had to wait for piped water in most areas until the 1960's. (In 1966, over 80% of all rural areas had no piped water). As flush toilets and septic tanks need piped water, it follows that very few rural houses had flushed toilets before that time. For a period in the sixties, and seventies, small grants were paid towards the cost of installing septic tanks; plans and specifications (which included a soak pit full of stones) were supplied by the Department of the Environment. Whilst septic tanks properly constructed to these specifications are adequate, the soak pit was not and has since been superseded by percolation systems.

Homeowners in the 60's and 70's who installed septic tanks according to specifications issued at the time should not be penalised now if the specifications have since been shown to be inadequate. The sensible thing to do for the future in order to ensure high quality sewage treatment is to set a target of upgrading all the older septic tanks over a period of say, 5 years. Grants should be provided to rural dwellers for this work in the same way as billions of pubic funds will be spent on upgrading urban treatment plants. The overall aspiration is the same, i.e. to eliminate water pollution by all sewage treatment plants.

In this way, public funds would be used in a fair and equitable manner to upgrade both urban and rural sewage systems.

Houses Also Die

By Dr. Seamus Caulfield

5 November, 2003

Between April 1st 1996 and March 31st 2002, 324,000 births were recorded in the State. The April 2002 Census showed that the population had increased by 291,000 since April 1996. If one were to argue that the missing 33,000 should be explained as due to **emigration** this would be to make the fundamental mistake of omitting to take into account the number of deaths during the six year period. When the 186,000 deaths are taken into account, the natural increase is 138,000 and the balance of the overall increase has to be due to net **immigration** of 153,000 in the six year period. Last week the ESRI Mid - Term Evaluation of the National Development Plan highlighted the fact that

over one third of all houses built in the State in the last five years were as variously described "second or replacement homes", "second/ replacement homes", "Second homes". In a later section of the Report, these are treated in the main as holiday homes in the countryside and the impact of these on the economy and on house inflation, in particular in the BMW region, is discussed. By Friday, the holiday homes were stated to make up 40% of all house construction in the last five years, this same percentage was repeated by another commentator in his column on Saturday and both commentators were cited in a political discussion on television on Sunday night. It is suggested that this demand for second homes has added 10% to the cost of houses, in particular in the BMW region.

Between April 1st 1996 and March 31st 2002, there were 268,604 house completions in the State but the Census of 2002 recorded an increase of only 164, 720 households since April 1996. To suggest that the shortfall of 103,884 new households indicates the construction of 20,000 second homes per annum is to make the fundamental mistake referred to in the opening paragraph. Because houses also die.

The main problem with the Evaluation is that it refers to the missing households as due to second or replacement homes when in fact the total is made up of two distinct components: (a) replacement houses for houses which have become obsolete and (b) the remainder which can be considered to be unoccupied second or holiday homes. Any attempt to estimate the holiday home component can only be considered when a best estimate is arrived at of how many of the houses in use in 1996 have gone out of use by 2002.

An erroneous depreciation factor of 0.005% (sic) of the housing stock quoted in Appendix 1 of the Evaluation, is unlikely to have been factored into the calculations but even the likely intended depreciation factor of 0.5% (approximately 6000 houses per annum) is almost certainly too low. Four

years ago, in its National Investment Priorities for the Period 2000 - 2006, the ESRI pointed to the historical experience of a requirement of 8000 houses per annum due to obsolescence or 0.6% per annum. It was estimated then that over 20% of housing would be required to cater of obsolescence. It is inexplicable why this element has now been so reduced four years later when house construction is more than 50% higher than the forecasts at that time.

One approach to disaggregate the obsolescence component from the second home component is to consider the inter censal changes in households in the five city boroughs, as these are unlikely to have a significant number of vacant holiday homes among them.

In the six year period between the Census', 41,358 houses were built in the five city boroughs but the 2002 Census recorded an increase of only 17,447 additional households. The missing 23,911 houses are not new unoccupied holiday homes but dead and probably demolished houses which were part of the 1996 total. This loss from a total of 261,444 in 1996 represents a 9% depletion over six years which is three times the estimate assumed by the ESRI. If even half this rate of depletion is applied to the housing stock in the remainder of the State, there has been a depletion of a further 38,780 houses in the six year period. The figure of 103,884 referred to above is therefore made up of two distinct categories (a) houses which have had to be replaced and (b) unoccupied holiday homes.

It can be seen from the above that the replacement houses are likely to exceed over 60,000 leaving a total of approximately 40,000 holiday homes constructed in the six year period, an average of less than 7000 per annum.

General Observations on Planning Policy for Rural Houses

Chapter Sixteen

Some suggested headings for a National Planning Policy.

1 *(a)* The policy must always respect our national history, traditions and culture.

   (b) Authority at all levels must be exercised by democratically elected representatives subject to appropriate auditing.

   (c) Considerations of health and safety must be borne in mind.

   (d) The constitutional rights of free citizens should be paramount.

2 *(a)* The policy should take advantage of our low population density and space available.

   (b) The overall objective should be to achieve continuity and balance as between urban and rural, East and West etc.

   (c) Citizens should be encouraged to become home owners.

   (d) No part of the country should be completely barred for suitable homes.

   (e) Optimum use should be made of existing infrastructure, roads, electricity, water supplies etc.

3 *(a)* All officials employed in the planning process should be graduates of an Irish training process which accepts the priorities of Irish culture, the democratic process and the constitutional rights of Irish citizens.

   (b) Un-elected officials cannot curtail property rights by arbitrary subjective decisions.

   (c) Rural residents should have at least equal rights as developers of holiday homes.

   (d) Objections to planning developments should be confined to permanent residents living within 400 metres of a proposed development.

Cathal McGabhann.

Locals only: *Jim Connolly*

Restricting planning in many rural areas to applicants who are either local or who are connected in one of a variety of special categories devised by planners to suit this restriction, is unacceptable in any guise or form.

(The reasons given to restrict the number of holiday homes or houses in the countryside in general are dealt with elsewhere in this booklet).

The main contention of the IRDA is that the `locals only' restriction is unconstitutional. A constitutional case may have to be taken in the courts on this issue. If it is proven to be unconstitutional, local authorities may be liable for compensation claims from planning refusals in the past.

Observations on the `locals only' restriction

- Ireland is now a multi-cultural society. Restrictions on constitutional rights based on race, religion, sexual orientation, disability and many other reasons are outlawed. Nonetheless, restrictions on where a person can build a house under the `locals only' regulation are based on the applicants place of birth and / or on his family connections and history. DNA testing in this regard may become a requirement in the future. How can any of this be justified under anti-discriminatory legislation?
- All development—past, present and future—in any given area is only possible because of the existence of human life.
- To deny the existence of human life is to deny development.
- To limit human life in an area is to limit development.
- Planning restrictions which exclude new blood coming into an area limit the potential for future development on many fronts, including social, cultural and economic development.

What a devastating impediment we live with in many rural areas where by the future of development of these areas is limited and shackled by planning diktat. Any one family or indeed any single individual can make a contribution to the area in which they live which can transform its development potential out of all recognition. So many examples of this natural occurrence exist in Ireland in art, literature, sport, music, commerce, job creation, tourist development—just to name a few, that the point is proven as it is made.

It is surely unjust under any interpretation of natural justice that the development of community life can be strangled by the `locals only' rule. This restriction makes a nonsense of the planners own official line—the proper Planning and Development of an area.

Viewed from a different perspective, the `locals only' rule bestows special privileges on local people by virtue of where they were born. This is also unacceptable in a democratic republic. Europeans fought long and hard in past centuries to break free from a type of society ruled by privileged classes who gained their powers to rule and govern by virtue of birth. For Irish people to allow any return to privileges as fundamental as the right to build a house (by virtue of birth) is madness.

None of the foregoing should be interpreted as either a lack of understanding or sympathy for the difficulties experienced by locals being refused planning in their own areas or on their own land. All citizens must receive equal treatment relating to constitutional rights in matters of planning. To use inflation in the cost of sites perhaps caused by `outsiders' as a justifiable reason for the `locals only' rule is to argue that two wrongs make a right.

The problem is planning

The cost of sites is governed by supply and demand. If you have ten people bidding on the only available site (whether they are locals or otherwise) the cost will rise. If on the other hand planning was available on ten sites to reflect the true need for housing, then a fair price would be available to all.

As long as an unjust planning regime is allowed to dictate which Irish citizens will have the privilege to sell a site or to build a house in this supposedly free country, the wealthy will always come out on top, while the rest—be they local or other wise—will continue to be denied the one privilege bestowed equally by birth on all Irish citizens, i.e. their constitutional rights.

Rural Housing Settlement Policy

Risteard O'Domhnall

County Development Plans and Regional Planning Guidelines should contain the following objective;

The council will facilitate the provision of single rural houses provided,

A They are occupied as the permanent residence of the owner or applicant for planning permission, for a minimum of three years from the date of completion. This time limit will not apply where force majeure circumstances exist, e.g. long-term serious illness, redundancy or family breakdown.

This objective should not include the areas in the immediate shadows of the five cities, gateways and hubs except where particular local circumstances exist e.g. where insufficient serviced land is available.

B They are subject to good practice in matters such as, protection of the landscape, groundwater and environmentally sensitive areas, design, location, road safety and do not generate ribbon development.

C The wastewater facilities are constructed in accordance with the EPA WasteWater Treatment Manual, for single rural houses or other appropriate system.
The planning authority will advise/help the developers concerned to comply with these requirements and not use them as a means of prohibiting single rural houses.

This objective is included for the following reason;
The provision of single rural houses is good planning and sustainable development and is in fact vital for Rural Development.

Sustainable Development is development that meets the needs of the present generation without compromising the ability of future generations to meet their needs. Rural housing policies that do not meet the needs of those of the present, or future generations, who wish to live in the countryside, are therefore unsustainable. Existing rural communities without additional houses are unsustainable, as development requires young vibrant people, who cannot exist in rural areas without additional housing. There will be no rural communities for future generations if current housing planning policies continue.

Social issues

A It is argued that group/village/town developments are more sustainable than one-off developments as people living in such groups live closer to local services like doctors, shops, pubs, etc. However, if those who provide these services cannot live in the countryside, then one cannot expect many of these services to be provided here. Also these services in turn need customers, who can only exist if they have houses in which to live, one depends on the other. It is current planning policies, which prohibit these services in rural areas.

B A certain critical social mass is necessary for healthy vibrant rural communities, including diversity of age, gender, background and profession. If only farmers and those who have economic ties to the countryside, as is basically the current position, are allowed to build houses in rural areas, then there will soon be very few living in rural Ireland. By 2010, it is estimated there will be only 10,000 full time farmers, 80,000-part time and 20,000 transitional. 8% approximately of these are female. Therefore current-planning policies will lead to an aged, male, very sparsely populated rural community which will ultimately die. Both urban and rural areas cannot develop without people. In the words of Bishop Jeremiah Newman "I would rather have people and problems than no people and no problems". What is development without people?

C Many feel that they can enjoy a much better quality of life living in rural areas, close to nature, surrounded by open space, with lower crime rates and greater privacy, etc. Why should the state decide that they cannot do so?

D It is estimated that one third of new houses are single rural houses. This does not take into account latent rural housing demand, i.e. those who wish to live in rural areas, but do not apply for planning permission because they know they will not get it. Therefore it is reasonable to assume that, the number of people who wish to live in rural Ireland is much greater than are allowed to do so. This big brother attitude is wrong.

Economic issues

A It is argued that high-density development requires less servicing per unit than single isolated development. It is more costly for the locality to service (with roads, electricity, telephones, postal services etc) one-off units than village/town housing. This is not correct. Houses already exist in the countryside, where these services already exist. In fact the opposite is often the case. Group housing demands many public services which rural housing does not e.g. public lighting, open spaces, street cleaning, traffic management facilities, new roads and public water and sewerage services.

B The more people live in rural areas, the greater the demand for services which, in turn, creates jobs. Building and maintaining houses would also create jobs in rural areas. This again creates demand for more rural housing, as more people will live in rural areas, nearer to their work, and with better local services, thereby enjoying a better quality of life.

C These extra people and jobs in rural areas would reduce the congestion, which exists in many of our towns. This congestion adds to the economic cost of most urban developments.

D Farmland is a capital resource. If some of it can be sold for housing sites, it adds to its value and brings capital into rural areas (reversing the normal flow of capital out of rural areas) which is again vital for rural development. One of the main problems of Irish Agriculture and the wider rural economy is that it is under capitalized. The sale of rural housing sites could become a much-needed source of capital, adding to rural regeneration.

E Sites in rural areas are often given free of charge to family members. Where they are sold, such sites make up 30% approx. of the overall cost of the house as against 50-60% in urban areas. Mortgage repayments are one of the biggest items of expenditure of most families. Cheaper sites would obviously reduce the financial pressure on them. More housing sites available in rural areas would increase the supply of housing sites, thereby reducing their price in both urban and rural areas. Therefore more single rural houses would be beneficial to both rural and urban people. They would help to make houses more affordable. Current restrictions on rural housing does not allow urban dwellers to buy a cheaper site in the countryside if they so wish, thereby adding to the cost of their house.

Environmental Issues

A It is argued that one-off developments are liable to do more damage to the landscape and groundwater than larger settlements. One-off housing generates septic tank seepage, disproportionate land-take, as well as, in many cases aesthetic blight.

These arguments are correct where bad development takes place, as has happened.

However such developments have got planning permission even though they should not have. However, all of these problems can be resolved if the houses are properly sited, designed, landscaped and if the waste water facilities are constructed in accordance with the EPA Waste Water Treatment Manual, for single rural houses, or other appropriate system. In fact many of these problems have arisen because planning authorities, where they do allow single rural houses, do not properly control such developments. The policy has often been strict prohibition or a free for all. This is not proper planning and sustainable development.

B The argument against using up agricultural land is utter nonsense. If current demand continues it would take about 2,000 years before this would happen. In fact there will now probably be a substantial reduction in agricultural output due to the Fishler reform of the Common Agricultural Policy.There is now a danger that agricultural land will in some instances become unused and derelict. Alternative uses for this land must be identified. Building houses on it could be one such useful use.

C Single rural houses are an inherent part of the Irish landscape and the traditional means of housing in rural Ireland for at least five thousand years. Continuing this tradition is protecting our heritage. It is also the traditional and current means of providing housing throughout much of the world, e.g. central Italy, parts of France Scotland Wales and Scandinavia etc.

D It is argued that under our commitments to reduce CO_2 emissions under the Kyoto Convention, that we should be reducing car dependency. It is easier to serve large settlements with public transport than urban generated one-off developments in the countryside. This is incorrect for four reasons;

1 The current public transport system is totally unsatisfactory.

2 Directing most development to urban areas has resulted in congestion in many of these urban areas.

3 Part of this argument involves, a) people travelling to work from rural to urban areas, and, b) rural areas being available to urban people for leisure pursuits

This seems to imply that planning is an instrument, which is used to bring people to work. Why not use it to bring work to people, as the National Spatial Strategy tries to do.

If it is environmentally incorrect to use private transport to get to work, surely it is even more environmentally incorrect to use it to go to the countryside for leisure pursuits. The logical outcome of this train of thought is incomprehensible.

4 Developing a comprehensive green energy policy would reduce CO_2.
Emissions, without reducing the freedom which the car provides. It would also provide an alternative use for land, create jobs in the countryside and reduce our oil dependency.

E Group housing leads to demands for public lighting. This lighting adds to public expenditure, increased consumption of electricity and creates light blight, which impacts negatively on the environment. Occupiers of single rural houses do not seek public lighting.

Normal recreational / artistic / hobby / personal development interests require space

The typical modern family with children will own a car or two, a buggy or pram, lots of clothes, children's and adults bikes, a child's swing, large toys, a dog and a cat, often a garage full of equipment and possessions associated with leisure activities or hobbies; a clothes line, perhaps a caravan, the list can go on and on.

Urbanisation/High Density living.

People who choose urban living have a right to do so. People who choose to live in the countryside must also have the right to do so.

Equity Issues

A It is a basic human right that people should be free to choose where they wish to live, subject to reasonable regulation rather than strict prohibition. People (whether they are from an urban or rural area), who wish to live in the countryside should have an equal right to do so as those who wish to live in an urban area. Planning is for all not just those who wish to live in urban areas. It is about facilitating development subject to proper regulation, not prohibiting it.

B Why should farmers be the only group in society who should not be allowed to maximise the value of their capital assets by selling sites if they so choose?

C Housing sites are an extremely valuable capital resource. When such sites are restricted to urban areas, only a tiny number of landowners benefit from their value. If single rural houses were properly allowed the number of landowners who benefit would be much greater. Also, as the number of sites available would increase, the price of sites would reduce, following the basic law of supply and demand. This would benefit both the buyer, (many of whom would now be non-rural people), and sellers. This would be beneficial to all of society.

It is argued that allowing urban dwellers to build houses in the countryside would increase the price of rural sites for the existing rural community. This ignores the fact that the current system of forcing people to buy houses in towns increases the price of sites in towns for the existing urban population. This is unfair to urban people or those who wish to live in urban areas.

D Most people wish to live in reasonable proximity to other people. It is morally wrong for the state to abandon those who live in rural areas to social isolation. This is the logical outcome of current rural housing planning policies.

The National Development Plan 2000–2006 states, regarding Rural Development, that *"The Government is committed to ensuring the economic and social well being for rural communities, to providing the conditions for a meaningful and fulfilling life for all people living in all areas and to striving to achieve a rural Ireland in which there will be vibrant, sustainable rural communities where individuals and families will have a real choice as to whether to stay in, leave, or move to rural Ireland".*

This can only happen if Single Rural Houses can be constructed.

Action Required

Councillors should include the above objective in their county development plans and regional planning guidelines. The Minister for the Environment Heritage and Local Government should be requested to include this objective in his proposed Rural Housing Planning guidelines.

Finally, "planning should be a problem-solving activity and the ideal settlement policy would be one which is responsive to local conditions and opinion and which considers all settlements regardless of their size. Planners must extend their attention and expertise to encompass social and economic planning as well as their traditional concern with land use strategies." *(Michael Pacione. Rural Geography)*

appendix

Is Housing in Dispersed Villages Sustainable?

Dr. Seamus Caulfield,
Ionad Taighde agus Staideir, Beal Deirg.

Like all development in Ireland, rural housing should be strictly controlled. There are certain areas where housing should not be allowed such as in extended ribbon development along main roads out of towns and villages. Along the western seaboard where dispersed villages are often separated by miles from the nearest neighbouring village, housing should not be allowed in the open (usually) bogland between, where there is no record of settlement in modern times. Broad but reasonable design and materials parameters should be part of the conditions attached to permission. There is no place in Ireland today for a free for all approach to housing. An equally extreme attitude is that there should be a ban on dispersed rural housing commonly referred to as "one off housing in the countryside" other than in exceptional circumstances. Unfortunately the argument against rural housing has been marked by a type of language completely inappropriate to a rational debate on a most important issue. Hyperbole, offensive descriptions of peoples homes, accusations of wrongdoing and not paying one's way, and even grossly offensive language directed at public representatives has marked the debate even by respected conservation bodies and environmental journalists in the national media opposed to housing in dispersed villages.

"Dispersed settlement is allegedly more expensive to service and maintain than concentrated settlement. But this is largely a fallacious argument in Ireland: we already have a heritage of dispersed settlements, which have decidedly intensified in the past 10 years. So unless we can JCB the existing pattern out of existence, it is there to stay" (Duffy, 1986,66)

The aggregate rural population of the State was 1.5 million or 42% of the total population in 1996. This was made up of (a) a quarter of a million people who live in all towns and villages with less than 1500 inhabitants but with at least fifty inhabited houses and (b) 1.25 million people who live in stand alone rural houses in dispersed villages. About one in ten of this number are farmers which means that less than one third of the households are directly associated with farming.

The breakdown of the 42% of the total population who are classified as rural is 8% in small towns and nucleated/street villages and 34% who live in communities of dispersed villages. The tradition of the settled dispersed community goes back at least five and a half thousand years in Ireland; four times longer than the tradition of nucleated settlement in towns or street villages. The total number of stand alone houses spread throughout the State is about 400,000 with a household formation rate of just over 3 persons per house. A very low erosion rate of 0.5% per annum is taken as the rate of decay/replacement demand. The main component of national housing demand of 50,000 new houses per annum for the next ten years is the increasing household formation rate rather than the projected increase in population. At the present household formation rate of about 3.0 , the number of new houses needed for the projected 360,000 increase in population is 120,000 or 12,000 per annum. A 0.5% replacement rate would require a further 6,000 per annum with the remaining 32,000 required for increasing household rate.

In discussing such statistics it is often easier to reduce the figures to more recognisable quantities. Consider what will happen in a small rural parish of 600 people living in 200 houses spread throughout a number of dispersed villages, if new housing is not allowed. Over the next ten years it can be expected that at least 10 houses will "die", usually with their last elderly resident. As the household formation figure drops towards 2.5, the remaining 190 houses will only accommodate 475 people, a population decline of more than 20% in 10 years. In order to maintain its population at its current absolute level such a parish will require 50 new houses to be built over the next 10 years. If the parish is to share equally in the projected 10% growth in national population over the next 10 years, an additional 24 houses will need to be built. Returning to national rural level, if housing in dispersed villages is not allowed, the inevitable result is that the one third of the Irish population who live in such an environment at present will decrease by about a quarter of a million people over the next ten years.

The most commonly voiced solution to the "problem" of new housing in existing dispersed villages is that new housing should be built instead in the towns and street villages. If the solution aims at allowing the rural population to maintain its share of overall population , the small towns and street villages would have to more than double in size or else new street villages would have to be created to accommodate 80,000 new households. The 1.25 million who live in dispersed villages in 400,000 households at present will require 500,000 houses as the household formation rate goes from 3.0 to 2.5, an additional 100,000 houses. If these were all located in the small towns and street villages it would more than double the number of such houses in a short time. Such a rate of growth would swamp the street villages and completely change the established relationship between the two settlement forms.

The case for attempting to put an end to the dispersed village tradition by fossilising it in its present state would only have validity if it could be shown that rural settlement was environmentally unsustainable in the long term. Arguments based on the tradition of nucleated settlement which pervades in England from Roman times or from Mainland Europe where the tradition goes back over seven thousand years has no relevance to the debate in Ireland. Six issues relating to sustainability have been raised in the debate about dispersed villages.
1. **Increased construction costs on the public.**
2. **Increased maintenance costs on the public.**
3. **Increased emissions of CO2 through increased use of car transport.**
4. **Depletion of finite land area**
5. **Depletion of agricultural output through loss of agricultural land**
6. **Depletion of natural habitat through loss of "natural hedgerows".**

Issues 1–3 have been dealt with by Brendan McGrath in a paper entitled "Environmental sustainability and rural settlement growth in Ireland" published in 1998 in Town Planning Review. He quotes a startling statistic taken from an earlier study by Mulvihill in 1984 "that it was about four times more expensive to build and service a house in the countryside that a comparable home in compact rural settlement and that the ongoing costs of maintaining a home in a dispersed pattern were between six

and 15 times the cost of maintaining a home in a compact settlement". There is in this statement an unfortunate confusion between building costs and the costs of providing services. The Mulvihill study (much of which is based on a still earlier study in 1975) makes clear that building cost differentials and some service differentials such as provision of electricity which were relevant in 1975, no longer applied in 1984. Mulvihill's figure, that the cost to the public for a new dwelling in a dispersed village was double that for a new dwelling in a compact village, was based on the cost of extending both the footpath and public lighting to the new dispersed dwelling. The public costs cited by McGrath relate therefore to the extension of street villages and towns and does not relate to the intensification of dispersed villages through the erection of new stand alone houses. When the irrelevant footpath and public lighting costs are removed, the cost to the public of the house in a dispersed village was less than 65% of the costs which apply in a street village or town.

The basis for the claim that the ongoing costs of "six to 15 times" higher for maintenance of a house in a dispersed village as against the costs in a street village which McGrath cites from Mulvihill simply does not stand up to scrutiny. Public costs identified by Mulvihill included "street lighting" which is given as ten times higher in the dispersed village than in the street village. In a dispersed village the street lighting cost is zero. Neither is there an ongoing charge for sewerage service included in the cost of the urban house. The only two public costs which are relevant today are school transport costs and postal delivery costs. Intensification of dispersed villages through new housing could be seen to lower the unit cost of providing school transport. Not all street villages have second level schools so that school transport could equally be a cost in such places. At any rate, school transport cannot be separated from overall education costs and it could be argued that because of the much higher rate of second level completion and third level participation in rural areas, there is a much higher return on investment in rural education than there is in urban education. Postal delivery costs are higher in rural areas than in urban. This is because the principle of uniform charge first established with the "penny black" in 1840 is still applied. What is often ignored is that the same principle of "postalisation" also applies to utility costs to the consumer such as the costs of gas and electricity which are normally sourced and generated in rural areas and provided, applying the penny black principle, to customers in cities remote from the point of generation at the same price as paid by those in close proximity.

The main component of ongoing costs to the resident of the dispersed village which Mulvihill identifies is that of commuting to work, school, church and shops which is calculated at £87 per urban household and £568 to £1543 per rural household per annum 1984. As the calculation is based on costs of over 20p per mile for car use, the figures quoted imply that the maximum commuting mileage by the urban dweller by car (even if other transport costs are zero) is 435 miles per annum. It is difficult to understand why McGrath chose to use such meaningless comparisons when his own study established that even with one hundred trains per week and well in excess of one hundred busses, car use per week in his urban households in Skerries at 334 miles per week, was not far short of the 435 miles per annum used above.

McGrath's thesis that rural housing was less sustainable than urban housing even if proven could not be applied to the country at large. Both the urban study (Skerries) and the rural area (The Naul and Garristown area) are situated close together in Fingal. The sample size is miniscule (31 rural and 32 urban households) and is atypical of the norm (household size 4.7 to 4.8). Seeing that journey diaries were kept only by those over ten tears of age, a difference of 1.0 year between the average age of rural and urban groups (11.5 and 12.5) may have been significant in particular as the average ages fall on opposite sides of a significant legal threshold of 12 years of age.

The most obvious problem with the thesis is that energy expenditure and other assumptions are taken from a study carried out in rural South Oxfordshire and "It was assumed that the South Oxfordshire and Dublin study areas were broadly comparable, that is relatively free-flowing road traffic...." In 1985, thirteen years before this assumption about Dublin's free flowing road traffic was made, Davy Kelleher, McCarthy reported in their study `Dublin in the year 2000':

"In Dublin, the huge increase in traffic volumes in recent decades has not been accompanied by major investment in new transport infrastructures. As a result, there is now all-day congestion in large parts of the city centre and peak-hour congestion throughout the greater Dublin area".

The main thesis which McGrath claims to have proven is that the rural household was responsible for 28% more carbon dioxide emissions than the urban counterpart. This would be correct only if one wrongly assumed that urban and rural emissions of CO_2 were similar over similar distances. As carbon dioxide emissions are directly related to fuel consumption, it is clear from such sources as that provided by the British Vehicle Certification Agency that urban mileage gives rise to between 50% and almost 100% more CO_2 emissions than rural mileage. When one applies the emissions differential to the car use figures used by McGrath, the result of his study changes completely with rural emissions being less than those in the urban.

Much more reliable statistical data than that contained in McGrath's miniscule and atypical sample from adjacent rural and urban areas in Fingal are available in volume 6 of the last Census. Comparisons between Mayo which has an 80% / 20% rural / urban population shows unexpected patterns of distances travelled to work and mode of transport used. It is clear from the figures available that even where public transport is available in urban areas well over 50% travel to work by car. In Britain which has a rural/urban population 10%/90% divide similar to Fingal, and a much more developed public transport system than in Dublin, 70% of workers still travel to work by car. As an assumed increased dependence on car transport is the main environmental argument used against dispersed rural housing, it is important that a thorough study of the real environmental cost of rural and urban car use be carried out to properly inform the debate about rural housing.

4 Depletion of finite land area.

It is argued by groups such as An Taisce that because the land area of Ireland is finite, that it is unsustainable to continue to build homes in dispersed villages. If one takes the extreme scenario that the State will have twenty years of house building at 50,000 houses per annum and that 35 % of those were to be built as stand alone houses in dispersed villages, what would be the impact on land? Assuming 0.2ha (half an acre) per site, the annual requirement for the 17,500 houses would be 3,500ha or 35 square kilometres. Twenty years of building at this rate would require 700 square kilometres. As the area of the State is just over 70,000 square kilometres, the impact would not come to even one percent of the land area. This does not mean that the entire area of a site is covered in concrete and tarmac, to use the emotive language often used by those hostile to dispersed villages. Houses with a footprint of 150 square metres and twice that area for a driveway and surrounding apron, will cover less than a quarter of the average half-acre site.

5 Depletion of Agricultural Output due to loss of agricultural land.

A national herd of approximately seven million cattle means that the State is about 1000% self sufficient in beef. A major export and until the 1990's the major one is nine out of every ten cattle produced in Ireland. If every one of the 350,000 houses to be built in rural Ireland over the next twenty years were built on good quality grassland they would deplete the grazing of 175,000 animals (at an average stocking rate of one per animal per acre) from total pasture resource. This depletion of 2.5% of the pasture land of our cattle herd means that instead of being 1000% self sufficient in beef, at the end of twenty years of building we would still be 975% self sufficient if alternative, more intensive production means was not employed to make up the shortfall.

(The depletion of Irish beef pasture and thereby reduction in the size of the beef herd has a positive effect in terms of our achieving the emissions targets of the Kyoto agreement. Every two half acre sites taken out of pasture for housing, means one animal less can be produced on the pasture. A grown animal belches very significant amounts of methane due to enteric fermentation in the rumen. In terms of global warming, methane is much more injurious than CO_2. Methane production from cattle is equivalent to over two tons of CO_2 per animal per annum. Every half acre site taken out of pasture for housing carries a saving of over one ton of CO_2 per annum. This is the equivalent of CO_2 emissions generated by approximately ten thousand miles of rural driving).

6 Depletion of Natural Habitat through removal of "Natural Hedgerows".

A "natural" hedgerow is a contradiction. As an environmental term, natural is used to distinguish the natural from the built environment. Roads, roadside boundaries and the hedges which may have been planted upon them are all part of the built environment. Roadside hedges are no more native than they are natural. The magnificent fuchsia hedge so common in Munster in particular is a South American plant introduced into Europe by a German botanist. It has been calculated that site clearance and setback for 17,500 houses per annum with road frontage of 30 metres would result in the removal of over 500km of boundary per annum. Over twenty years this would amount to the removal of 10,000km of roadside boundary. However, for every 30 metres of roadside boundary removed for a stand alone site, every 0.2ha site will have in excess of 150 metres of new boundary created, an increase of over 500%.

A simple condition of any permission for the construction of such a dwelling could insist on a similar boundary to that removed to be incorporated into the line of the new boundary.

Many of those who argue against new housing in traditional dispersed villages take as proven the claim that rural housing is unsustainable environmentally or else quotes statistics from now out of date scientific papers which have established this "proof". It can be seen from the above that the proof does not always stand up to scrutiny. It is a reasonable conclusion that the most unsustainable thing about rural housing is the case which is made against it.

The case for De-listing An Taisce

Dr. Seamus Caulfield,

The controversy over An Taisce's role in planning has again flared up with the decision of Mayo's County Councillors to call for the removal from this body of their designated status under the Planning Act. I support fully the decision by Mayo County Councillors on the very real grounds set out below that this once highly respected body has forfeited its right to the position of responsibility granted to it by the Department of the Environment.

I empathise that strict planning laws are essential, that there are many places in Ireland where houses should not be built and that where they are allowed, reasonable parameters of design and colour could be included in the conditions attached to the permission. In particular ribbon development on the outskirts of towns needs to be strictly controlled. In places like Mayo where dispersed villages are separated by miles of unoccupied land where there is no record of habitation in recent times, these areas should be preserved free of housing. Anyone demanding a free for all does not deserve to be listened to. But neither does An Taisce now deserve the right to be listened to because of its extreme attitude in relation to rural settlement which is unsupported by valid statistics or other research.

There are at least three reasons, any one of which could be considered sufficient for An Taisce to be de-listed.

The first reason is that An Taisce has demonstrated in its own publications, an explicit prejudice in relation to national and rural planning. Its headline "The National Spatial Strategy: an Irish Oxymoron" published last summer while the National Spatial Strategy was in the process of being drawn up is explicit proof of prejudice on its part. An Taisce's declared opposition in principle to almost all dispersed rural housing negates the critical role it should play in planning applications, all of which should be considered on a case by case basis.

The second reason is that An Taisce has demonstrated what, on the most benign interpretation, can only be described as extreme carelessness in publishing grossly erroneous statistics in relation to housing in the Greater Dublin area and in the rest of the country. In attempting to prove that a very high percentage of houses constructed outside the Greater Dublin Area are "one off houses in the countryside" it states:

"36% of new housing is in the countryside. Of this 80% - 90% is one off. The problem is even more acute than this figure suggests, since more than 50% of housing is built in the Greater Dublin Area, very little of which (1%) is one off".

These figures are simply erroneous. The percentage of houses built in the Greater Dublin Area has declined from 41% in 1966 to less than 32% in 2000. The percentage of one off houses in considerably higher than 1% in the Greater Dublin Area and in fact this is one area where a real problem may exist. Elsewhere in the same document it is stated "The daily encroachment of urban-generated housing into the countryside is measurable as is the reduced number of families living in towns and villages". This again is erroneous as there is no evidence to show that the overall number of families in towns and street/nucleated villages is declining.

The third and most compelling reason of all is that An Taisce refuses to accept that the term "village" has a wider meaning in Ireland than it does in Britain and that in this country it includes the sraidbhaile or street village, the clachan or nucleated village and the baile fearann or dispersed village. At the last Census in 1996, the population of the Greater Dublin Area was 1.4 million. The 2.2 million in the rest of the State was evenly divided between those who live in other cities and towns of at least 1,500 together with those who live in small towns and street / nucleated villages totalling 1.1 million and 1.1 million who live in dispersed villages. One third of the total population of the State and half of the population outside the Greater Dublin Area live in dispersed village communities. But according to An Taisce, these people do not live in village communities but live instead in "one off houses in the countryside". As average household size decreases from its current level of approximately 3.0 per household to an expected 2.5 per household over the next decade, and even if only 5% of the housing stock was lost through obsolescence during this decade, An Taisce's proposed ban on rural housing would result in a massive decline in the predominant form of rural settlement in Ireland and the one which has the longest tradition stretching back into prehistory. As only 10% of the population of dispersed villages are classified as farmers, the expectation for farmers which An Taisce is willing to make is irrelevant. The refusal of An Taisce to recognise the predominant form of rural settlement in Ireland and the disgraceful response of using abusive language to a Minister of State instead of entering a debate on the issue, shows clear evidence that this body is not prepared to listen to any other viewpoint which is at variance with its own perceptions.

One third of the population of the State live in dispersed rural villages and should not be subjected to accusations by self appointed judges of being both parasites and being selfishly anti-social. "If communities or house builders had to pay the true costs—economic, social and environmental—of their one off houses, the phenomenon would disappear overnight".

"The most disturbing aspect of this process is that those who selfishly pretend to be unaware of the consequences will actually get away with it within their lifetimes".

In a county such as Mayo where seven out of every ten people in the country live in dispersed villages and as such are the recipients of these abusive and accusatory comments, it is entirely understandable that the public representatives should have responded as they did to An Taisce. One can only hope that the decision by Mayo County Councillors will lead to this once fine organisation which was An Taisce, entering into a rational debate on this most important issue of maintaining our traditional rural settlement patterns and by doing so may regain the high respect in which it was once held.

Planning & Rural Housing
Local Authority Interpretation of
The Planning & Development Act 2000
(as amended)

---

*The Resultant Effects on the Market &
Recommendations for Future Action*

*Submission by the Irish Auctioneers & Valuers Institute
to Mr Martin Cullen T.D.
Minister for the Environment & Local Government*

May 2003

CONTENTS

1. INTRODUCTION

The 1,600-strong Irish Auctioneers' & Valuers' Institute has observed the seismic changes in planning in rural areas and sets out herein its views in relation to planning controls on rural sites and housing, in particular one-off homes.

This submission includes observations on special planning conditions and reasons for refusal in relation to:

Planning & Development Act 2000
Regional Planning Guidelines
Chapter III Part II
Part III Control of Development

Part XIII Amenities
* Areas of Special Amenity
* Landscape Conservation Areas

This submission also refers briefly to the probable impact on rural planning of Common Agricultural Policy Reform III, which is due to be passed into law next year.

Rurally located estate agency practitioners were asked to assess the impact of the Act in their own locale. Extracts from some of their comments and anecdotal evidence is included in this submission.

'The Republic guarantees religious and civil liberty, equal rights and equal opportunities to all its citizens and declares its resolve to pursue the happiness and prosperity of the whole Nation and all of its parts, cherishing all the children of the nation equally...'
Poblacht Na hÉireann - Irish Proclamation, Easter 1916

2. BACKGROUND

This Submission is set against the current problems of housing availability and affordability, as well as the long-established, continuing and escalating withering of Ireland's rurally based population. 70% of Planning Applications in Ireland are for one-off houses / sites in rural locations. It is the view of the IAVI that a blanket ban on one-off housing prevents many individuals from building their own home at an affordable price.

Retired U.C.D. Professor Séamus Caulfield, an academic and archeologist affiliated to The Irish Rural Dwellers' Association, referring to current Development Plans / Acts, has stated that they do not cater adequately for the majority of our "population, who live in scattered villages". He particularly criticises local authorities for "blocking the building of summer homes in rural areas" and claims "authorities appear to consider them in much the same light as others would a brothel. Better that people are spending their money in this country than in the Costa Del Sol", he stated.

Professor Caulfield also states that to deny reconstruction and building in rural locations in Ireland sets out to move the majority of the population into urban areas, contrary to the Irish settlement heritage, in effect resulting in "the decommissioning of certain townlands".

Some counties and Gaeltacht areas are seen to clearly segregate as a matter of policy, as enshrined in the Act.

Rural rights campaigner, Jim Connolly, claims that Clare County Council imposes planning restrictions that "will transform the west of the county into a great desert, devoid of people" where, he states, "only farmers and their immediate family can get permission, sometimes, to build in the countryside."

Current policy denies retirees, or prospective holiday-home dwellers, the right to build in parts of Clare and in most other coastal / rural counties. In a paper on the Céide Fields in Co. Mayo Professor Caulfield said, "Rural developments dating back to the Stone Age were dispersed throughout the Irish countryside but, in recent years, planners were using the British Anglo-Saxon planning model that emphasizes settlement in urban areas - nucleation settlements". He argues that this model is based on the urban population being 90% whereas, in Ireland, 40% of the population is rurally based. "One-off rural housing should continue, but it should not be a free-for-all" he concluded.

John Greer, a senior lecturer in the School of the Environmental Planning at Queens University in Belfast, believes that "one-off rural housing reduces the demand for public sector housing and helps to regenerate rural areas."

John Ducie, Vice Chairman of An Taisce holds that "the increase of such developments prevented increases in the critical mass of rural town and village populations, which is necessary to attract inward investment, employment, industry and tourism." He conceded, however, "there should be one-off rural housing where there was a pressing social need, or where family members are working on farms or family activities in the area."

In the Spring 2002 Edition of the IAVI's quarterly publication, The Property Valuer, Kevin Heanue, an economist at Dublin City University Business School wrote:

".... (Recent) changes to the existing regime of one-off rural housing would appear to be inconsistent with two main objectives of current housing policy, by not only removing the most affordable housing option for large sections of the population, but also contributing to social segregation in housing. Any new regime must directly address these inconsistencies or else the objectives of housing policy should be changed"

3. CURRENT POSITION

Despite the wishes of many local authorities to the contrary, one shoe does not fit all. There is no single solution that can apply to all areas and all applicants. However, that must not prevent the creation of an effective and consistent national policy that allows for identifiable and reasonable local considerations.

With so many planning authorities at liberty to adopt their own policy on the rural housing issue, the picture countrywide is very much an inconsistent patchwork, even in immediately adjoining locales, where different authorities hold sway.

There is inconsistency in how local policies are enforced, which is not helped by evident mobility within the planning profession and by

the use of planners whose professional and social background is not indigenous to this country, let alone the region in which they are practicing.

The planning regime is undermined by a failure to properly police planning conditions, from occupational restrictions (some solicitors, as a consequence of the lack of enforcement, occasionally convey without regard to such conditions) to conditions requiring that new units be properly finished, including landscaping and external finishes. Breaches of the latter elements frequently cause unsightly blight in the countryside.

The IAVI suspects that while many local authorities impose occupational and related restrictions, even though serious doubts may apply to same in legal / constitutional and EU terms, not all such authorities have sought to enforce such conditions. It is not unreasonable to ask: do these authorities actually see such conditions as enforceable? If so - and if legal - they should be enforced. If not, they should never have been imposed in the first instance.

The IAVI believes that a consistent and logical policy must be adopted by both central and local government on this issue, which would be applied on a uniform basis in each area, having regard to specific but reasonable local needs. Against the background of planning arguments, we must not lose sight of the economic impact on the rural community and farming in particular. Farmers had become used to selling on the odd site in order to raise cash in times of need, such as for the education of children. Agriculture is already facing a bleak future and what is effectively a blanket ban on one-off housing will worsen the plight of the farming community in the immediate future.

It is probable that some legal challenges to the decisions of local authorities may be made. Such decisions have had a tendency to evolve on an ad-hoc basis and have not been based on any evident central policy. It is as if authorities are seeing how far they can push the boundaries, before someone feels sufficiently aggrieved to cry 'halt!'

The questionable denial of both civil and E.U. rights, by preventing both anyone from outside an immediate area and others in specified categories, from securing planning permission tarnishes the name and image of Ireland as the country of the

welcomes and may, in time, bring the State into conflict with the European Commission.

Planning "pre-conditions" being suggested by local authorities include:

* That the applicant be living in the area / locality (questionable on Constitutional and E.U. grounds)

* That the applicant is the son / daughter of the landowner (in some instances, only one member of a family is seen by the local authority as having an entitlement to planning for a house and all others are refused permission)

* That the applicant is employed in the area (which excludes the retired and unemployed)

* In Gaeltacht areas, that the applicant speaks Irish (questionable on Constitutional and E.U. grounds)

* That the applicant gives an undertaking to the local authority that he/she will guarantee occupancy of the eventual dwelling for 5/7/10 years (apart altogether from the proper enforceability of this condition, it impacts in a major way on the open transferability of title and, thus, on the security on offer to a mortgage company, undermining the ability to borrow for the provision of what should be an affordable home)

* Restriction on the use of a dwelling house as a holiday / retreat home (this condition may well prove to be unconstitutional)

4. SPECIAL AMENITY AREAS

The IAVI recognizes the need to protect areas of Special Amenity and Landscape Conservation Areas from widespread ribbon and one-off housing developments. The concern of this Institute is that the current regime, which has developed on an ad hoc basis in recent years, uses this legitimate concern to impose a blanket ban that extends to the greater portion of our countryside, which does not have such scenic or historic importance. This 'sledgehammer to crack a nut' approach is causing widespread damage to our rural economy and threatening the demise of our country lifestyle. Put simply, if the reasons for a blanket ban were so compelling, would the opposition to the current regime be so widespread? It is time to introduce some rationality into our planning regime and our rural housing policy.

Special Amenity and Landscape Conservation Areas should be included in local development plans as locations where one-off housing will not be permitted, save in exceptional circumstances, the definition of which should be left to the Department and not to individual local authorities.

In the interest of equity and access to affordable housing, owner-occupied one-off housing should, in principle, be acceptable in all other locations, providing bio cycle waste disposal is used, mains water, communal water of a proper standard, or acceptable well water is available and ribbon development is not allowed to become a norm. When permission is being sought for single houses, applicants should be asked to provide, where possible, three or four sites, with shared access and services. Thus, the applicant ends up with further sites that can be made available for others to construct affordable homes. While economically it may make sense for these additional sites to be sold to other parties, we do not believe that this can be an actual condition for planning purposes. Such minor clustering should not mitigate too strongly against the desire for the 'one-off' home, as small groups of 3-4 homes will still be in a totally rural environment. They should, with the use of bio cycling, also enhance sustainability.

5. COMMON AGRICULTURE POLICY REFORM

It is widely acknowledged that the current review of the Common Agricultural Policy will have a major impact on rural settlement in Ireland, with the outcome almost certain to be less supportive of the traditional Irish rural lifestyle than was heretofore the case.

At a time when such a major external factor is likely to mitigate against a viable Irish rural economy and rural lifestyle, it is incumbent on the Irish Government to ensure that domestic policy is designed to sustain both the rural economy, even with its diminished importance to Ireland's GNP, and rural lifestyle. A countryside effectively bereft of farmers may well result from further CAP reform and such an eventuality will undoubtedly expedite the depopulation of the Irish countryside.

However, we simply cannot allow domestic planning policies to simultaneously prevent repopulation of our rural areas, when there are individuals who wish to live in such locations.

Managed growth enhances sustainability. An effective blanket ban on one-off rural housing is a cumbersome and counter-productive management tool. Rural living can and will be enhanced by bringing more people to live in the traditional scattered villages of Ireland. We should not examine whether this should be encouraged but, rather, how it will be encouraged. While much of the modern Irish town planning system was imported from our nearest neighbour, one has to question the consequences of some of its aspects in the Irish context - in particular the limitation of eight houses per acre in urban developments for decades, which was surely a major contributor to our housing crisis.

An even more alien import is the concept that all rural dwellers must be forced into small urban areas.

6. COMMENTS RECEIVED FROM IAVI MEMBERS INCLUDED THE FOLLOWING:

"Before the famine in the 1840s, the population of this country was in excess of 9 million. Today, we struggle to house 4 million. How can we expand if rural areas, traditionally places of abode in this country, are no-go areas for building?

It was always my opinion that the Planning Authority was concerned about structures and their design, as opposed to who was allowed to live in a certain area. With the implementation of this new policy, the Planning Authority has become the demographic watchdog, dictating who will live where and who will have to live at home with their parents in the country for the rest of their lives, if they wish to remain in their own locality. I recently had a client, a farmer, seeking to build three houses on his 200-acre farm for three of his family, five miles out in the countryside. After twelve months of discussion, the planners gave him two houses. The third member of the family must stay at home. Wasn't there a nursery rhyme in relation to this about three little pigs?

It has become policy in the last five years to push the population into the small villages, rather than leave them in the rural areas in 'one-offs'. In this immediate area we have 4-5 such villages, which have been granted planning permission for quite large estates. One such village had c. 45 houses five years ago, and is now heading for c. 170 units. There is no mains sewer system, a poor mains water supply and it is located on an extremely busy main road -

surely problems for the future. As I say, there are 4-5 such villages in this area alone.

Another such example, being prohibited from development because of the policy, is an old famine village, which is now privately owned. The planners will not allow the owner to renovate and preserve the area. The ruins as they stand will fall into further disrepair and eventually be lost. Is this proper planning?" Eamonn O'Neill B. Comm. MIAVI, O'Neill Estates, Kinsale, Co. Cork

"For about three years, we have been endeavouring to sell a residential development site for 14 bungalows between Lahinch and Liscannor. The site is part of a larger site, sharing services and road access, which was developed as part of the Seaside Resort Scheme. Our site has a condition that the dwellings be used as permanent residences. We have not been able to sell as a result. There is no local market for principal residences on this particular site." Paddy Darmody FIAVI FRICS FSCS, Sherry Fitzgerald McMahon, Ennis Co. Clare

"The decrease in the supply of one-off rural sites / smaller newer houses in the market has been dramatic in recent times. This is increasing prices for both sites and 'starter' rural housing. If the trend continues under the present legislation, supply will continue to fall. The sale of the one-off site with Outline Planning Permission by smaller farmers was viewed in rural areas as a form of financial assurance in times of need, but has now almost entirely dried up. Recently, some clients have even tried, out of frustration, to sell an acre or two without Planning Permission, to stave off economic hardship, knowing full well that the chances of getting Planning Permission are almost nil." Eddie Barrett, FIAVI, North's Estate Agents, Tralee, Co. Kerry.

"In County Kildare, a relative of mine and his sister applied for two separate planning permissions to erect dwellings on adjacent sites on family land.

* The decisions to grant one and to refuse the other were issued on the same date

* Both houses were of the same design

* In their decision to grant, Kildare County Council recommended a shared entrance

* Right across the road, a neighbouring family obtained two planning permissions for two children.

* Condition number two of the decision to grant includes a five-year occupancy clause."
Edward Carey FIAVI, Enfield, Co. Meath

"The late John Healy, in his book "No One Shouted Stop", published in the 1950s, wrote lamentingly about the depopulation of his native County Sligo. That his warning was not heeded is evidenced by the fact that, in the last five years alone, nine GAA clubs in the county have amalgamated into four clubs, due to falling family sizes and a falling number of households in rural areas. In one north county area, three clubs had to amalgamate into a single unit to produce anything viable.

Farm representatives have for many years cursed the afforestation of large areas of rural Ireland in the period 1970-2000. As these plantations mature, rural Ireland has yet to see any of the jobs that were promised in association with thinning and harvesting, or follow-up industries. On the contrary, as I travel the roads of County Sligo all I see is third-class roads damaged by the hauliers, as they bring the logged timber to Scariff and Waterford. Even the harvesting is done by machine.

Two secondary schools amalgamated into a single school in Tubbercurry and in Tourlestrane, an amalgamation of four primary schools into one is currently under active consideration, for the same reasons that caused amalgamation of the sporting clubs.

We need various types of rural housing - dispersed rural housing and clustered settlements.

If planning is granted with conditions and compliance with those conditions is enforced by the Planning Department, then what is the problem in permitting well designed houses that are both socially needed and environmentally friendly."
Roger McCarrick MIAVI of McCarrick & Sons, Tubbercurry, County Sligo.

7. CONCLUSIONS & RECOMMENDATIONS

Conclusions

Sooner rather than later the Government must amend the Act and deal with matters which clearly:

o Undermine the traditional market forces that affect selling / supply / demand

o Prevent the establishment of any meaningful counter-flow, of those willing to live in rural areas, to the depopulation that has been underway for decades and that will be accelerated by the impending CAP Reform Proposals, due to be adopted in 2004.

o Create economic hardship for farmers

o Prevent many prospective home-owners from providing affordable housing for themselves

o Will embarrass Ireland in Europe, if successfully challenged by the European Commission

o Will embarrass central and local government in Ireland if successfully challenged in the courts.

Recommendations

Specifically, the IAVI recommends that Government should:

1. Examine the most recent census with a view to identifying depopulation blackspots.

2. Liaise with sporting bodies, the churches and the Department of Education to analyse the real impact, at local level, of underlying population-related trends.

3. Ensure the creation of a UNIFORM policy towards rural housing that reflects the diverse needs of different localities.

4. Ensure that planning conditions are fully enforced.

5. Prevent the widespread misuse of the planning process via groundless objections.

6. Question the role of An Taisce, in adopting such a vehemently negative stance in this area across the entire country.

7. Promote, through the planning process and regulations, wider use of bio cycling for drainage disposal, consequently enhancing sustainability by reducing the use of septic tank drainage.

8. For one-off owner-occupied housing (regardless of the connectivity of the occupants to the locality) ensure that proper standards are imposed and enforced and that shared accesses are encouraged, while otherwise restricting

development only on the following grounds:
a) Adverse impact on a Special Amenity or Landscape Conservation Area
b) Inadequate water provision, or foul drainage solution
c) Serious traffic problems.

9. For holiday homes, ensure that they are erected in clusters, close to services and with approved group water and drainage schemes, in locations other than Special Amenity or Landscape Conservation Areas.

10. Extend and encourage the Rural Resettlement Schemes.

11. Extend the Rural Renewal Tax Designation provisions to the many areas not yet included.

12. Give priority to less-populated areas in the provision of one-off housing.

13. Examine the practical and academic background of planners operating in rural Ireland in order to ensure that planning is sympathetically controlled for local communities and is not, as at present, frequently divorced from the concerns and needs of such communities.

14. Encourage planners to meet and liaise with local communities to a much greater extent than at present.

15. Give consideration to the provision of grants and/or interest-free loans to private developers who are prepared to enhance the mains water, surface water, or foul sewerage disposal systems in villages. A developer, who might build an additional say 20-30 houses in a village, would undertake the work involved, but the improved infrastructure would benefit the existing population, while leaving open the possibility of additional houses being provided in the future. Such a provision, where there was an evident and immediate benefit to the local community from a new housing development, might well help curtail some of the groundless objections to planning applications.

APPENDIX

IAVI TASK FORCE MEMBERS:
Eddie Barrett FIAVI (Past President IAVI) -
        Convenor
Peter Tuohy FIAVI MCIArb (Vice President IAVI)
Edward Carey FIAVI (2002 North Leinster
        Regional Council Chair of IAVI)
Donagh Dougan MIAVI (2003 Munster Regional
Council Chair of IAVI)

The Draft County Development Plan 2003 (Kerry)

Sean O' Donoghue
23 July, 2003

The ongoing discussions concerning the Draft County Development Plan remind me of Seaffraidh O' Donnchadha an Ghleanna who wrote 'An Reacht thar Tuinn'. This poem was written after 1661 when the Cromwellian planters were confirmed in their holdings. Its opening verse may be translated as 'This law from across the sea is the ruin of the noble Irish people by wrongfully taking our possessions and depriving us of our rights to all Ireland'.

The officials of the Planning Authority emphasise that a rural settlement policy will not stand up unless an occupancy clause is imposed as a condition of the grant of permission in rural areas. Even the opinion of Senior Counsel has been received stating that such restrictive practice is lawful under a section of the Planning and Development Act 2000. If applied generally some meaning and sense could be made of it but it would not be workable. Having regard to the basic concept that all our citizens should be cherished equally the provisio is constitutionally inept, inappropriate and unacceptable. Neither will the proposal be acceptable to the European Commission. Members of the Council were issued with a resume of Counsel's opinion but keeping the full text under wraps is considered divisive and inconsistent with the advocated policy of transparency in planning. My requisition for a copy of the entire text was met with denial. Granting permission for a dwelling and then restricting its use to a person of a particular class or description should not be adopted. This would be equivalent to a system of categorising people in sets based on social and economic status, a people that would be socially disenfranchised by class. Ear tagging may become an essential element of enforcement and traceability. The councillors must ensure that this provision is excluded when voting to adopt the County Development Plan.

There is a deliberate campaign to exclude ruinous houses and obvious sites of former houses from the benefit of planning permission for reconstruction under the Rural Settlement Policy. This is a coordinated attempt to impose an alien planning programme on rural Kerry and to inter forever the historical remnants of our forgotten forefathers. It seems the conflicting attitudes are contradictory when our heritage is destined to oblivion while the relics of imperialism acquire legislative protection.

Councillors are being coerced into believing that the current level of housing development in the countryside is unsustainable and cannot continue indefinitely. Show me the man with a specific qualification in rural planning and I will talk with him. Certainly migrant planners brought directly into the system could have no appreciation of the subtle factors encapsulating the Irish rural ethos. For thousands of years the greater Irish population lived in the countryside. Dispersed forms of housing existed long before the advent of urbanisation. Down the ages our committed ancestors managed and moulded the landscape with care and affection.

Rather than restricting housing development in the countryside there is a positive case for freeing it from the shackles now being experienced. In 1841 the Irish population of 6.529 million people lived in 1.329 million houses with an average household size of 4.9. In 2002 3.917 million people lived in 1.288 million houses with an average of 3 persons per dwelling. It is projected that the average household size will drop to 2.5 within a generation so that 1.567 million residential units will be necessary to house a population of the current size. The latest available statistics indicate that in 1996 we had 669,422 urban based houses while 453,816 were in the countryside. The figure for the countryside includes towns and villages up to a population of 1,500. It seems therefore that a deficit of at least 500,000 rural homes exists compared with 160 years ago. If current policies are pursued the rural housing stock will fall further.

An important minimum requirement is that the planning authority should encourage people to inhabit the backlands. In the short term the REPS partially addresses the need to protect and manage sensitively the legacy of our beautiful countryside. In the light of new CAP proposals decoupling poses a significant and serious threat to the mountainous regions. Sheep may be removed entirely facilitating an environmentally orientated disaster leading to irreparable distortion of the flora-fauna regime. Abandoning these beautiful areas will leave nobody with the interest or incentive to maintain them. We will be facing into a time warp that will rapidly spiral out of control.

The councillors as a whole are sympathetic to the rural cause and have generated a new level of respect for their positions. Without their valuable input detrimental restrictive practices would continue to be inflicted on unsuspecting country people. It is a pity that planning officials in order to implement draconian measures indulge in spinning policies designed to confuse and demoralise those elected to adopt the County Development Plan.

Removing the occupancy clause will be a major step in the right direction. The adoption of the IRDA submission in its entirety is vital but many other factors must be addressed which merit inclusion. Let us all in unison, give the councillors direction and assistance in the field of our greatest concerns and establish a rural settlement policy that will be a beacon on the template for sustainable preservation of an orderly and aesthetically developed countryside.

IRDA Public Statements
Press Releases, Dail Questions & Public Statements

Press Release

UK Influence on Rural Planning Issues.

The Irish Rural Dwellers Association established a year ago to unite rural people in the face of mounting pressures on the future of rural communities, have exposed what may well be the main cause of refusals for houses in the open countryside and corresponding pressures to move people into towns and villages. Reaction against the entire planning regime as if affects rural houses is countrywide and large turnouts at IRDA meetings reflect the hurt, frustration and anger of ordinary people who can't build houses for their families - often on family owned land.

"The planning regime is undemocratic, anti-people and out of control" says a spokesman for the IRDA. "A root and branch change is now essential including radical legislative change".

Pointing out that the traditional Irish housing pattern based on the townland (baile fearann) stretching back thousands of years which is uniquely different from England and mainland Europe, has become almost entirely dominated by an English planning philosophy, the spokesman said that the IRDA are determined to see control of planning policy brought back to elected Irish politicians.

Until recently, Town Planners educated in Ireland graduated without any rural qualification. Available journals and planning literature are predominately English. Most graduates are accredited by the Royal Town Planning Institute (RTPI) in London. In addition, many Irish planners received their education in colleges in England.

Speaking at a public meeting in Macroom (23/6/03) Kieran Lynch, ex senior planning executive and consultant lecturer, agreed with Jim Connolly of the IRDA, that the Irish Planning regime is UK influenced. "We have failed to produce an Irish planning philosophy so far" he said.

In An Bord Pleanalas' annual report for 2001, the Chairman John O Connor states that the majority of extra resources (including 50 planners) brought in to cope with the increased workload are UK based.

As well, the RTPI have set up an Irish Planning Policy Panel with an office in Clare. A discussion paper published in July 2002 is intended to influence Irish Planning Policy. The RTPI have only three regional branches worldwide i.e. Scotland, Wales and Ireland. When asked the reason for their Irish Planning Policy Panel (they have no other such panel outside Ireland) a spokesperson for the RTPI in London said "because of the long historical links between England and Ireland, because they don't really consider Ireland to be `abroad' and because they have so many members working in planning authorities in Ireland".

Jackie Healy Rae T.D. raised a Parliamentary question on this issue. He was told by the Minister for the Environment and Local Government on 20/5/03 "My Department did not have any role in sponsoring or financing the (RTPI) documents preparation and publication". The IRDA interpret this to mean that a private English professional planning body are conducting a serous maverick operation to influence Irish Planning Policy. "This is outrageous in a country with its own proud cultural heritage which supposedly is no longer part of the British Empire".

"This is not a case of Brit bashing - The IRDA would be equally opposed to an alien planning philosophy being imposed on the Irish people from Germany, France or any other country" the spokesman said.

Individual planners have huge powers of personal discretion in recommending permission or refusal for houses. Inconsistencies abound everywhere. Concern for Irish culture and traditional rural community life is completely ignored in the current regime. It is further largely undermined by an influx of planners from many other countries around the world who make decisions in Ireland without any understanding of Irish traditions and without being obliged by the D.O.E. to do any course whatsoever in Irish history or related subjects before being allowed to practise here.

The IRDA believe it is a small wonder that rural people and people wanting to live there are suffering, frustrated, angry and demanding change. They have lost all respect for planning authorities and see them as the successors of the landlords who tried to depopulate Ireland in the 19th Century.

It is a very serious matter for democracy when people loose respect for institutions of the State or state sponsored private bodies like an Taisce. These institutions cannot function in the long term in any democracy without the respect and support of the tax payers who pay their wages.

The IRDA are running a Conference on "Positive Planning for houses in the Open Countryside and Vibrant Rural Communities" in Caherciveen on the 3rd and 4th of October 2003. Details are available at 065 9058229.

Dail Questions Nos. 406/407

Chun an Aire Comhshaoil agus Rialtais Aitiuil To the Minister for the Environment and Local Government

To ask the Minister for the Environment and Local Government, the person on whose authority a group (details supplied) was employed to set up the Irish Planning Policy Panel, under a person (details supplied) to work on formulating rural settlement policies here and to produce a discussion document. The New Rural-Urban Relationship, A Framework for Discussion, dated July 2002; and the cost implications to the taxpayer.

To ask the Minister for the Environment and Local Government when the responsibility for formulating the rural settlement policies in Ireland was handed over to the Royal Town Planning Institute of London; if there is a reciprocal arrangement in place whereby the Irish Planning Institute has a role in formulating rural settlement policies in England; and if he will make a statement on the matter   - Jackie Healy-Rae.

For WRITTEN answer on Tuesday, 20th May 2003.

Ref Nos: 13622/03 and 13623/03

Reply

Minister for the Environment and Local Government (Mr Cullen)

I propose to take Questions Nos. 406 and 407 together.

I understand that the document referred to was prepared by Royal Town Planning Institute's Irish Planning Policy Panel as a discussion document, seeking views on key strategic issues for rural planning in both the Republic or Ireland and Northern Ireland. My Department did not have any role in sponsoring or financing the documents preparation or publication.

Rural settlement policies in Ireland are a matter for the Government, and for regional and local authorities, with overall Government Policy in this regard having been set out in the National Spatial Strategy, which was published on 28th November 2002.

Dail Question No: 218

To ask the Minister for Finance, the Department which funded the Rural Settlement Policies in Ireland: and if he will make a statement on the matter   - Jackie Healy-Rae.
For WRITTEN answer on Tuesday, 27th May 2003.

Ref No: 14537/03

Reply

Minister for Finance (Mr. McCreevy)

I understand the Deputy wishes to know if any Exchequer funding was provided to the Irish Planning Policy Panel, in connection with a paper prepared by that group entitled: The New Rural-Urban Relationship, A Framework for Discussion. The Irish Panel is a regional branch of the Royal Town Planning Institute, which is a private professional group dealing with planning issues and is based in the United Kingdom. To the best of my knowledge, no Government department had any role in the commissioning, financing or the publication of the above paper.

Expenditure on Rural Affairs, which mainly relates to rural development, is funded by the Department of Community, Rural and Gaeltacht Affairs.

Press Release:

Compensation claims on Planning Refusals — Are they on the way?

In September 1997, Clare County Council received a report entitled `Criteria for the Evaluation of Landscape Quality' prepared by CAAS (Environmental services) Ltd., which was used as a basis for the evaluation of landscape quality in the county. The Council had commissioned the report as they considered it would be beneficial if they had a more concrete set of procedures in arriving at landscape designations in its review of the Development Plan.

In the preamble to its report CAAS discuss the relevant part of the 1963 Planning Act "Preservation of views and prospects and of amenities of places and features of national beauty or interest (Part IV(7), 3rd schedule (519) L4 (PD) A 1963", and as part of this discussion, obviously deemed in prudent to make the following observations.

The object of this legislation is faced with difficulties because: -

It seeks to "preserve" (prevent change) a landscape which always has and always will change.

It assumes that there are fixed reference points as to what constitutes "features of natural beauty" when in fact these vary from individual to individual and from time to time. This analysis also highlights the legal insecurity of any development control measure - such as designations on account of "natural beauty" - which could limit the development rights of private property. It is inconceivable that designations on the grounds of "natural beauty" alone could be legally justified as being based upon judicious, replicable, objective or equitable criteria.

Whereas, on the face of it, it may appear extraordinary that a company compiling a report establishing the criteria for the Evaluation of Landscape Quality which was destined to be used in the assessment of planning applications in Co. Clare should feel it necessary to say "It is inconceivable that designations on the grounds of "natural beauty" alone could be legally justified", etc., it could be assumed that CAAS were just being careful in protecting themselves from any legal responsibility, regarding the uses to which the report would be put by the Council.

Having thus stated their professional opinion on the legal aspect, the CAAS report goes on to detail the methodology used to arrive at mapping the Zones of sensitivity under the five headings i.e. Vulnerable, Sensitive, Normal, Robust and Degraded.
In general, planning decisions for houses in rural areas are hugely influenced by classifications on landscape Quality as they are designated in the County Development Plan.

The question arises however, as to whether individual members of Clare County Council or the Council as a body where made fully aware at the time of the serious reservations expressed by CAAS on the legal insecurity aspect of its report.

The full report was probably available to Councillors at the time of its publication in 1997, but did the Manager or Chief Executive Planner of the time highlight the legal warnings expressed by CAAS to the Council - that is the question that is now being asked by the IRDA.

One way or another, the Council may well be exposed to almost unlimited litigation and claims for compensation if it can be proven in the courts that planning refusals based on designations of "natural beauty" or similar cannot be legally justified as CAAS has indicated in its report.

It would also appear that the legal insecurity aspect would apply to all other planning authorities in the country where similar designations based on features of national beauty apply. All these other counties may find themselves exposed to massive compensation claims as well.

Public Statement 18/7/03

Ref: Response by Liam Conneally
to the Irish Rural Dwellers Association Press Release.

I refute the suggestion by Liam Conneally that I distort the context by quoting the section where CAAS highlights the legal insecurity aspect.

Mr Conneally implies that legal insecurity risks only exist in the "absence of an objective assessment of the landscape". He further implies that because CAAS provide "the information on the landscape in an objective and coherent way etc" that this alone is sufficient to eliminate the legal insecurity aspect.

In my reading of the CAAS report, as an average layman, I can find no claim whatsoever by CAAS that the information they provided eliminates the `legal insecurity' aspect which they themselves highlight in Sec. 2.

On the contrary, they include a number of other passages in Sec. 2 and Sec.3 which would appear to be of far more value to anybody taking a case against the legality of the Councils designations than in their defence.

Examples: Sec.2: " Visual issues are only one small part of a wide range of issues which contribute to the character or distinctiveness of a landscape"

Sec 2 : Also quoting EPA guidelines "... examining responses which are felt towards the combined effects of new development. This topic is complex because...attempts to scientifically measure feelings and perceptions are not reliable".

Sec.3: Limitations: "This report does not attempt to define the scenic quality of different parts of the country as it is very difficult to arrive at agreement on the mappable extent of scenic areas, There appears to be no objective means of defining the limits of physical and topographical features which go to make up a scenic area". (This statement seems to clash with Liam Conneallys contention that CAAS information on the landscape is objective).
All the above examples taken from the report appear to bear out and justify CAAS's own substantive statement on page 4 *"It is inconceivable that designations on the grounds of `natural beauty' alone could be legally justified as being based upon judicious replicable, objective or equitable criteria.*

To the layman, the legality of the Councils designations of Visually Vulnerable etc which are widely used in some areas of the country to refuse planning permission seems to be founded on very shaky ground.

The traumatic effects on people of planning refusals cannot be over stated. On a case by case basis, they take away the national rights of Irish people to build permanent homes, to sell sites and to allow new families into depopulated areas. Refusals threaten the very survival of vibrant communities in beautiful rural and coastal areas.

Gauging the growing feelings of anger and frustration of ordinary rural people country wide, it seems inevitable now that legal actions will be taken against some local authorities and by extension, An Bord Pleanala. The CAAS report may be the very key that unlocks the floodgates.

IRDA

Comparisons between An Taisce policy and that of the Government on rural housing.

Written evidence from An Taisce policy papers compared with Government publications and statements show that there are clear differences of policy between these two bodies on rural housing. In some instances the differences are so stark as to be contradictory.

In this situation it is not just extraordinary but also fundamentally unjust that this private organisation continues to exercise a statutory role in the planning process.

Large numbers of planning applications referred by local authorities to An Taisce (under Statutory obligation) end up being refused. Of the planning decisions to grant approval which are appealed by An Taisce to An Bord Pleanala, about 95% of the appeals are successful.

Government Ministers, T.D.s and Senators openly criticise and condemn An Taisces' role in planning for rural houses.

To the ordinary taxpayer it appears that we have two governments - one elected by the people and a private one elected by nobody. A primary reason why people united under the banner of the IRDA was that they feel totally let down by our Governments inability to protect us from the policies and influence of An Taisce.

An Taisces policies also play into the hands of County Managers and the planning regime in general - all of whom are determined to impose urbanisation on the Irish race.

It is against every principal of democracy that a private organisation which openly proclaims policies contradicting government policies both in the spirit and in practice should have a statutory role in overseeing the implementation of those same government policies.

Extracts from An Taisce Policies on the Rural Built Environment
* "Although Irelands approach to its rural built environment is unsustainable..."

* "Outside of such settlements (rural villages and towns)...new residential construction should be limited to those...(whose) job connects them to the land...or for reasons of compelling social need in order, for example, to take care of elderly or sick relatives".

* "An Taisce supports rural development, though not one-off housing development in the countryside".

* "In its approach to new development in the countyside An Taisce is animated by sustainability. This embraces social, economic and environmental criteria. One - off housing generally fails under each of those headings".

* "The policy (An Taisces') does not permit housing for commuters or those who cannot show that they will engage in a significant element of land-based activity".

* (Eco-Villages) "Apart from walking, bicycles and public transport, shared transportation modes such as people carriers should be the norm. Implementation of the strategy should be monitored annually by the relevant local authority". (An Taisce are promoting dictatorship, not democracy)

* "One off housing in the countryside, particularly urban generated one off housing, is generally against the public interest because it is unsustainable - economically and socially as well as environmentally and often aesthetically. It is a particular problem in Ireland".

* "New one off housing should not generally be permitted".

* "One-off housing generates septic-tank-seepage, light pollution and disproportionate land take as well as, in many cases, aesthetic blight".

* "The viability of alternatives including in every case the possibility of building...in nearby towns and villages should be investigated...in most cases the economic, social, health and even community infrastructure in towns and villages is superior".

* "Where local residents...fail to get planning permission on their land, the possibility should be investigated of local authorities providing village housing at cost".

* "One off...development...tends to be less sustainable than high density development to high design...in cities, towns and villages".

* James Nix (An Taisce) states `The infrastructural levy would be reduced...for the replacement of one story houses with five story town houses'.

Summary: Throughout, An Taisces policies reflect a sustained attack on new rural housing which, by definition, house the people who make up rural community life. Their policies promote the alternatives of enforced urbanisation and villagisation on rural populations.
Less that 8% of the population are engaged in farming and this number is reducing all the time. This decline coupled with An Taisces policy of limiting new rural houses to people connected with the land guarantees the end of rural community life.

There is ample evidence in rural areas all over Ireland that depopulation caused by a number of factors is already a serious threat to the future of many communities. Whereas the end result of An Taisces policies will be the virtual depopulation of the open-countryside, government policy as expressed in the White Paper on rural development, in the National Spatial Strategy and in statements by An Taoiseach and Government Ministers is for the retention and development of vibrant rural communities in the traditional settlement pattern of the townland or dispersed village. This will be pursued in parallel with the development of towns and villages.

Nowhere in An Taisces policy, is reference made or recognition given to the traditional settlement pattern of the baile fearann or townland and its importance in the cultural history of rural community life. Indeed the only place where the word culture is used by An Taisce is in the context of rural architecture.

The real cultural history of rural Ireland, which is centred on the people, merits no consideration whatsoever.

By contrast, all Government policies stress the importance of preserving and developing this rich, cultural heritage. This can only be done by keeping rural communities alive with new families and this in turn cannot be achieved without building new houses in the open countryside.

Government policy and An Taisce Policy are completely incompatible on these issues.

Government policy and statements on rural housing and community life.

* 'Characteristics of Rural Ireland' - Examples. Strong identity of rural communities, especially cultural, linguistic, heritage and sense of community.

* Dispersed nature of rural communities.

* Policies...directed towards improving the physical, economic and social conditions living in the open countryside.

* Programme for Prosperity and Fairness (PPF) "...will contribute significantly to integrating the strategy for economic and social development of rural areas..."

* ...Rural proofing underlines the need for future policy measures...appropriate to the needs of rural communities.

* ...rural development policy has become identified with countering those socio-economic processes which are considered responsible for decline...

General Considerations
* The majority of rural dwellers are neither farmers nor directly dependant on farming.

* In the long term, the relative economic significance of farming will decline.

Ministerial Statements:
* "...this Government is fully committed to the development and prosperity of rural areas"

* "People want the right to live in rural Ireland ...a right endorsed absolutely clearly in the White Paper...planning policy should, as far as possible, facilitate people willing to settle in rural areas..."

* Overall Government strategy...most importantly, preservation of culture and heritage of rural areas..".

* "...without young people in a rural community, it will wither and die".

* "Arguments on the grounds of sustainability put forward against rural housing and development in rural areas often have no firm basis in reality".

* "...there is not, and will not, be a ban on rural houses".

* "We have come a long way...from a position where there were strong proposals to limit rural housing to farm families, to a clear Government Policy...that will sustain rural life".

National Spatial Strategy.
* "In Ireland there is a long tradition of people living in rural areas. This strategy...supports sustainable rural Ireland".

* "Overall...to sustain and renew established rural communities..."

* "...to ensure that rural settlement policies take account of and are appropriate to local circumstances. *(Surely, population decline with knock on effects on school closures, loss of services etc is a local circumstance prevailing in rural communities in most rural counties)*

IRDA—To all elected Representatives:

Ref: the two faces of the Royal Institute of Architects of Ireland (RIAI)

Following on my last communication to you dealing with An Taisce, I enclose herewith excerpts from published sources concerning another private organisation, The Royal Institute of Architects of Ireland. This institute made a submission to the Joint Oireachtas Committee on Environment and Local Government on 6/11/03 on rural housing. The following excerpts from RIAI papers submitted to the Committee clearly show that they are strongly opposed to building "one off" houses in the open countryside. (See section A of this letter).

They highlight issues such as sustainability, use of the car and water pollution as arguments against "one off" houses and instead promote living in towns, villages and clusters of houses. As a professional and highly influential body, The RIAI, are entirely free to present their point of view.

But is it their only point of view?

In section B of this letter are excerpts from a different publication currently on public sale i.e. 'Build Your Own House and Home', published by House and Home, in association with the RIAI. If your compare the excerpts in section A with those in section B you may be forgiven for asking - could it possibly be the same RIAI or are there two of them in the country promoting opposite points of view on rural housing?

Section A:

RIAI submission to the Joint Oireachtas Committee on 6/1//03. Presented by Toal O'Muire, - then President of the RIAI.

Excerpts:

"RIAI housing policy 2002.....reinforcing existing towns and villages as sustainable settlements instead of allowing unsustainable scattered peripheral housing".

"...the future cost of servicing these (rural) houses...may cause these houses in turn to be unaffordable and perhaps even abandoned..."

"...the aggregate effect of dispersed one-off housing is to burden our children with unsustainable...costs".

"...unsustainable costs of scattered peripheral housing in social, economic and environmental terms..."

"The RIAI wants to ensure that...inadequate architectural quality (is) classified as a non-compensatable reason for refusal of planning permission".

"Clustering of houses could provide solution to debate over one-off houses"

"Lots of people from our cities and towns unconnected with farming, have bought one-off rural sites...this not only weakens the life...of towns or villages but exerts unnecessary strain on public services". (Quotation from Toal O'Muire - RIAI president)

"Where possible...living accommodation...encouraged through 'living over the shop' incentives...in smaller towns and villages".

The full text of the RIAI submission is with the Joint Oireachtas Committee.

Section B:

Excerpts from "Build Your Own House and Home" (Published in association with the RIAI).

"If you are thinking of building your own 'House and Home', take inspiration from this countrywide selection of exceptional one-off houses, designed by members of the Royal Institute of Architects of Ireland".

The `countrywide selection' referred to, is a pictorial record of 9 new houses.

8 of the 9 are located in rural and coastal areas of scenic beauty. (one in Mayo is a seaside holiday home featured on the front cover).

Average size; 2112 sq. feet/
Average planning time; 5 months.
Average style; modern.

Apart from the 8 houses featured above, the book also details case studies of several other new houses in rural areas; two in Kerry, one in Clare, four in Cork, one in Wicklow. By comparison, there are only a couple of case studies in suburban settings.

Excerpts continued:
"Escape to the country. Many urbanites harbour dreams of a retreat to the quiet life of the country and more and more are making that dream come true.; One such couple found peace and tranquillity in the Cooley peninsula and even managed to build their dream home".
(Their story as well as many others, is illustrated with beautiful pictures of rural scenery).

Summary:
Almost the entire thrust of the 336 page book deals with different aspects of building "one-off" houses in the country - for example - there are several pages each on septic tanks, group water schemes, finding sites, planning difficulties, alternative building techniques etc. - all in a rural context.

No mention to be found in this book of the negative aspects of "one-off" houses so strongly put to the Joint Oireachtas Committee by the then President of the RIAI Toal O'Muire.

The Book ends with a list of about 300 RIAI registered architects who "specialise in the design of one-off domestic houses". Amongst this list of eminent professionals is this firm

OMS (O'Muire Smith) Architects.
Milltown House, Mount St Annes,
Milltown, Dublin 6.

Mr. Toal O' Muire can be contacted at this address.

Conclusion:
The IRDA fully support the concept of good architectural design. It is up to the Architectural profession to sell themselves to the public as they do so well in the book discussed here. Currently, "the percentage of architect-designed homes in Ireland is in low single percentage figures" according to "Build Your Own Home". The only problem the IRDA have with the RIAI - and it is an extremely serious problem - is the way in which they openly use their professional weight and prestige at conferences and at the Joint Oireachtas Committee to criticise and condemn ordinary people wishing to build in the country while they themselves shamelessly tout for similar business amongst the wealthy.

Throughout history Irish people have had to put up with elitist groups lecturing us on what is good for us—the cant never varies "Don't do what we do, but do as we tell you".

Rural people are no longer on bended knee.

Yours sincerely,

_____

Jim Connolly
Acting Secretary
IRDA

Housing and Democracy

There is growing pressure to limit people's right to build houses where they want to live. Instead established homeowners and a range of activists (all mostly city based) want to dictate where and what type of dwelling people should live in. This is dressed up as being "in the public interest", "pro-environment" and some other such platitudes. It is fundamentally undemocratic. The purpose of this note is not to argue for the abandonment of every planning principle, but to widen the debate on the entire issue.

In any discussion on housing policy there will be many sides to the arguments, however, to date practically all the discussion has been one sided against the rights of people to build in a non urban context. Is it the wish of society that we depopulate the countryside? Should everybody live in cities towns and villages? Who is to decide this question and what are the consequences?

To begin there are a series of issues that need be taken into the equation, notably: -
- Density of housing and population
- Population imbalance
- Local infrastructure to provide employment
- Social issues (crime and culture)
- The purpose of the countryside
- Technical issues (pollution and traffic)
- Profit on land sales

Density
Ireland has one of the lowest housing and population densities in the developed world, as the table below shows.

Table 1 European Land Area & Population

	Land Area	Population	Density
	SQ. KM.	(000)	000/Km2
AUSTRIA	83,850	8,139	97.1
BELGIUM	30,510	10,182	333.7
DENMARK	43,070	5,357	124.4
FRANCE	547,030	58,978	107.8
GERMANY	356,910	82,087	230.0
IRELAND	70,280	3,917	55.7
ITALY	301,230	56,735	188.3
HOLLAND	37,330	15,808	423.5
PORTUGAL	92,080	9,918	107.7
SPAIN	504,750	39,167	77.6
SWITZERLAND	41,290	7,275	176.2
UK	244,820	57,833	236.2

Source: Geographica. The Complete Atlas of the World

Ireland has the lowest population density, at 56 persons per square kilometre, thus the arguments about the impact of extra dwellings on the countryside of rural house-building are of limited impact. Taking the C.S.O. population projections for the most optimistic set of circumstances for 2011 at 4.255 million persons, this would give Ireland a density of 60.5 persons, still well below the next nearest country. As all the persons must live in some form of dwelling the density will not change to any great extent in the next 10 years, the island is under-built by the standards of Europe.

Table 2 European Housing Stock

	Land Area	Housing Stock	Density
	SQ. KM.	(000)	000/Km2
AUSTRIA	83,850	3,790	45.2
BELGIUM	30,510	4,661	152.8
DENMARK	43,070	2,509	58.3
FRANCE	547,030	29,275	53.5
GERMANY	356,910	37,250	104.4
IRELAND	70,280	1,362	19.4
ITALY	301,230	26,526	88.1
HOLLAND	37,330	6,710	179.7
PORTUGAL	92,080	N.A.	N.A.
SPAIN	504,750	19,582	38.8
SWITZERLAND	41,290	3,606	87.3
UK	244,820	24,600	100.5

Source: Euroconstruct.

As table 2 clearly shows Ireland with less than 20 dwellings per square kilometre, is half of the next lowest country, Spain. Do their housing densities ruin these countries? It can be strongly argued that they do not, and can be further contended that the pattern of housing is a definite part of a national identity. Thus one expects to find bungalows in Brittany, coastal apartments in the South of Spain and along the Riviera. Ireland has always had a dispersed pattern of rural dwellings, it is the Irish landscape. To now implement policies to stop this form of continuous development is to change the Irish identity. Such a change in policy should not be brought in without a national debate on the use of the countryside. The statistics in tables 1 and 2 clearly show that there is no pressing need to adjust current practice on density grounds. We are under housed and spacious. The notion that rural housing will take a disproportionate part of the land mass is not borne out by the facts. Thus there already exists a substantial rural population, but current planning restrictions and objections to developments are hampering this evolution. The most recent census of population shows that there is a large imbalance in the population as between the East and West coasts. Thus the development of the whole infrastructure outside of the eastern seaboard might well be a priority for the future. How is this to be done? By forcing people to live in clusters, in the towns and cities or in the open spaces.

Population Imbalance
Table 3 Irish Population Trends

	1966	2002	+%
Leinster	1,924,702	2,105,449	9.4
Munster	1,033,903	1,101,266	6.5
Connacht	433,231	464,050	7.1
Ulster (part)	234,251	246,571	5.3
State	3,626,087	3,917,336	8.0

Source: C.S.O.

It is quite encouraging to note the continuing increase in the population, since 1971 there are almost an extra 1 million people living in Ireland. The fastest growing region was Leinster, with over 9% growth between 1966 and 2002. Leinster now accounts for 53.7% of the State's population, while Dublin alone holds 28.7% of the entire population. Leinster continues to outgrow the rest of the country and has been doing so now for over 30 years. This has led to a concentration of resources in this area, and brought with it all the associated problems of traffic, development and rising land prices.

To change this policy will mean getting employment into areas outside Leinster, as without jobs people will not want to live there. This implies that planning authorities must be prepared to zone land for factories and offices and provide housing for the expected inflows to follow. There is not a vacant stock of dwellings ready to be occupied, thus a building programme must emerge. The question is where is this influx of people to live? in cities and in towns?, or repopulate the countryside. The countryside that is so cherished by the environmentalists has to be maintained. Hedges have to cut, weeds kept at bay, houses have to be painted. Subsistence type farming will not do this task, as many are below the national average income, and not so inclined towards this type of activity.

Local infrastructure

As mentioned above, to encourage resettlement will involve changes in the overall-planning context. The lack of developed land and vacant housing in many areas is a constraint on new developments in rural Ireland. The E.S.R.I. medium term forecasts show a demand for approx. 45,000 dwellings per annum. It is technically possible to do this with large scale Ballymun type projects, however the lessons from this latter experiment and the experience in the UK and elsewhere, would show that this is not the way to go about solving housing crisis. Every Local Authority is required under the 2000 Planning Act to prepare a housing strategy as an integral part of the development plan, and that this strategy should be reviewed every two years.

The current "favoured" solution is to select various villages and towns and develop these, with clusters and other types of housing. Has any research been carried out on the impact of such enlargements on the culture and scale of these smaller areas? What will be the local impact of housing a quantity of people in a small community that was a reasonable unit prior to the "invasion"? In the UK some new towns were built (Telford/Milton Keynes), which turned into soulless places, with no centre and no tradition. Policy should not be directed so as to swamp or destroy the local culture, but work with it.

Social Issues

In general terms there is less crime, less vandalism and less anti social behaviour in rural Ireland than in urban Ireland. Also there is greater social integration, with dispersed settlements people tend to play and meet more often, especially at parish level. For general quality of life it is clearly understandable that parents would wish to rear children in such an environment and they are apparently prepared to live with the journey to shops and schools for this style of living. Given how recent the population has become urbanised, the closeness to the rural roots of the majority on the island is still very deep. The general good interpersonal contact that exists in Ireland between people is a distinctive part of our culture and identity, and marks us out from many of our European neighbours. Living in a rural environment can also develop an independence of character, which is quite conducive to good neighbourliness and good order in society. Extra families living close to small communities do not over burden that community, but provide the

new blood to help regenerate, to make viable the schools shops and local sporting teams etc. It preserves the parish without making it a town.

It has been claimed that letting people build outside the urban areas leads to more traffic. On certain roads this is probably true, but it appears that there will be no difference in vehicle ownership whether the person lives in the town or the country side, as in either case there will be same amount of car ownership and density of cars. Almost every person now aspires to a car and they are everywhere. Thus the urban rural split will not have much impact here.

Our great sporting tradition, especially in the GAA, is firmly based on the parish and on a series of local clubs. These are the backbone of the game and need a constant supply of young people to keep this alive. They are the unpaid and often un-sung hero's who provide activity for our children. As any parent will admit, if the children are active in sport, then they are unlikely to be hanging around or engaging in anti social behaviour. To deprive communities of new blood will eventually lead to the demise of certain clubs, and encourage centralisation.

What is the land for?

What is the purpose of the Irish landscape? A vacant series of hills and valleys! to be visited by foreign and urban tourists? or a place for people to live, grow and mature. How are we as a nation to decide on the pattern of settlements? Let un-elected pressure groups like An Taisce decide? Or ask/guide the people or their representatives. This topic needs a broad discussion at many levels, let the planners set out their objectives bearing in mind the Irish culture, let the sociologists come up with proposals on the pro/anti urban theories and let the local representatives be consulted on their own communities. It is only natural that people wish to live where their families have resided for generations, among their kith and kin, where they are known and feel at home. This may sound like wishful thinking, but it is apparent, that a sizeable proportion of our people wish to live otherwise than in an urban context. Given the low density of both our population and housing, surely this aspiration can be accommodated with sensible local approaches. The prospect of Ireland becoming a rural museum is not an attractive one.

Technical issues

There can be no excuse for polluting the land with ineffective septic tanks and ad hoc sewerage treatments works. This is an area where professional engineers can provide the solution in conjunction with the local authorities. Properly installed and maintained septic tanks or local treatment systems can and should be insisted upon and policed. If people want to live away from established sewerage systems then they cannot be allowed to add to contamination and therefore they must be prepared to sign up to a clean area policy. A proper system of building inspection under the Local Authorities / Homebond should oversee this and no excuses accepted. Placing people into towns that already have overloaded sewerage systems and lack of tertiary treatment works is almost the same as allowing people to build ineffective septic tanks. There is also a sewerage problem in urban Ireland as many treatment works are not up to standards. Two wrongs do not make a right, the septic tank is a potential and real problem, but there are solutions that need to be policed.

Profit on the sale of land

Since the Kenny proposals were never adopted and since land for house building has not been taken into public ownership, then it is inevitable that profit will be made on the sale of this land. If and when this land is sold, it has to be legally transferred and all such transfers are under the control of the State. Thus there is no black hole where there is no scrutiny to tax, and capital gains tax if it arises will be levied. Any such revenue forms part of the overall state revenues and is available to public funds. As it is private individuals who are prepared to pay farmers for a site, this is not a drain on public resources. Also many of the sites are transfers to the children of the owners and the question of profit does not arise here.

A vibrant building industry gives extensive employment to architects, engineers, builders and producers of building materials. Economists will introduce the concept of opportunity costs, that such resources might be more effectively employed else where, but the reality on the ground is that real employment is given, real materials are used and the cost of housing is borne by the individual. Would it be preferable that people built or bought property in Spain France or elsewhere and helped those economies rather than the local economy. This is the Keynesian system at work and not some econometric model.

Summary

Ireland is under-built and under populated by any standards. Ireland has a tradition of dispersed rural dwellings, which are part of both the Irish landscape and culture. The countryside is not a museum to be visited by foreign and urban visitors, but a place to live, grow and mature in a caring community. There are technical solutions to septic tanks and pollution problems, but they need effective planning and policing. Car ownership will be the same whether people live in a rural or urban context. There appears to be social advantages to rural living. There may be less crime and vandalism, and given the preference of the many families who wish to rear their children in a non urban context, it seems sensible to continue the type of housing practices that have stood the test of time. In this regard there is no need to allow building at every site and cross - roads in the countryside, many areas should be left untouched. Also sound planning practices should not be abandoned, e.g. skylines should not be broken, buildings kept off main roads and other well established rules. There is still a lot of space out there to accommodate peoples' desires.

Joe McDonnell
September 2002

The Editor
The Irish Times
D'Olier St.
Dublin 2

Re. Debate on Rural Housing
12th. Sept 2002

Dear Sir,
I have been following aspects of this debate in the columns of your paper and elsewhere now for some time, and feel that there has been quite a one sided argument advanced. My thoughts are set out in the attached paper, which I would like to submit to you for possible publication on the issue. Basically I do not want to see Ireland become a "rural museum", preserved for urban and foreign visitors. I believe that a dispersed pattern of housing is an essential part of the Irish identity and landscape.

If you require any clarification on this note, I would be pleased to be of assistance.

Yours sincerely
Joe McDonnell

Irish Rural Dwellers Association
Submission to
the Department of the Environment
Heritage and Local Government on
Draft Guidelines sustainable rural housing

Presented: 29th April 2004

Setting the context: Housing Guidelines — an historic document

The Guidelines under review are the single most important development in planning for rural houses in decades.

* Country people are in turmoil over planning; they have lost all respect for this institution of the State.

* The Guidelines, if adjusted at this juncture to address vital areas of concern identified in this IRDA submission, have the potential to have a profound effect for good not alone for rural and would be rural dwellers, but for Ireland as a whole.

* Basic civil rights to housing, to freedom of movement within our country, to choosing a personal quality of life, to designing our own houses, to developing our own property and many other fundamental rights have been eroded and are now fully controlled by an authoritarian, sanctimonious and holier than thou planning regime.

* The depth of hurt, injustice and victimisation felt by so many decent Irish citizens who love and cherish the countryside will not be alleviated by anything other than a root and branch change.

* It is most important that the final Guidelines are not perceived as a ploy of simply tinkering with the present system. This would do nothing but increase tensions.

* At heart, the issue is a territorial one (wherein mans deepest emotions live) and if the planning regime has anything to learn from Irish history, it is that resistance to injustice relating to property, to attempts at social engineering and to denial of human rights is deeply ingrained in the national psyche of the Irish people and will not, nor could not, be suppressed.

* In a modern democracy, constitutionally motivated people power is emerging more and more as a legitimate protector of human rights; the newly found voice of a united rural people must be listened to in this modern context.

* People were part of the living landscape of Ireland for thousands of years before the first Planning Act of 1963; while always acknowledging the traditional generosity to our neighbours rights and to the Common Good, Irish people are demanding balance and common sense in planning and will no longer accept having their civil rights and personal choices being overwhelmed by planning diktat.

The foregoing, in the view of the IRDA, is a fair reflection of the current situation in the country vis-à-vis Planning refusals for rural houses.

Back to Basic Principles

* Gradually, since the implementation of the first Planning Act of 1963, basic civil rights of many people wanting to build houses in the countryside have been curtailed or denied. An urban / rural divide has been created wherein restrictions on freedom of movement and on private property etc imposed on rural dwellers do not apply and probably would not be tolerated by urban dwellers

* A foreign planning philosophy of forced urbanisation and villigisation is being imposed. Example: An existing Draft County Development Plan says "...The countryside ...(policy)...to restrict residential developments...". Elsewhere the Draft Plan predicts "...a need for 1,463 new houses a year in the County..." Taken together, these two statements amount to forced urbanisation. This policy is reinforced by zoning land for building in rural villages only.

* The results of forced urbanisation can be seen all over the country in the form of incongruous detached and semi-detached suburban estates swamping traditional villages.

Seeking Justice:

The new Guidelines should reinstate democratic planning principles: All people must be treated equally.
Planning decisions should:
(a) Be seen to be under the complete control of elected public representatives.
(b) Respect the constitutional rights of all citizens and comply with the spirit and letter of Government policy.

(c) Acknowledge falling populations due to changes in agriculture.

(d) Promote and foster the resettlement of depopulated areas by non agricultural as well as agricultural families.

(e) Acknowledge that all people make a contribution to their community whatever their occupation / profession or way of life.

(f) Have regard to Irelands position (unique in the E.U.) of having suffered a 50% decline in population in the past 160 years and of having the lowest population density per sq. kilometre.

(g) Have regard to Ireland having the lowest housing density per head of the population in the E.U.

(h) Reflect the need to preserve a balance between rural and urban populations.

The National Interest:
An age of building:

* Arising from a unique combination of circumstances, Ireland at the end of the 20th and the beginning of the 21st Centuries is experiencing an upsurge of building of all kinds which is unprecedented in our history.

* This age of building is clearly in the national interest.

* In housing we are seeing an end to sub-standard accommodation as opportunities are created for tens of thousands of ordinary citizens to build high quality houses.

* This window of opportunity in our times must be exploited to the benefit of as many people as possible. Circumstances outside of our control may close this window at any time.

* New housing built today will not alone raise the quality of life of the present occupiers but will ensure a high quality of life for future generations.

Benefits to the economy:
* The construction industry in general is playing a major part in fuelling our economic success.

* It is unjust that rural areas which in many cases have seen little evidence of the Celtic Tiger, are also denied multi million Euro investment in local economies because of planning refusals. People do not make frivolous planning applications to build houses. In virtually all cases they have their finances arranged and are ready to build if approved.

* Example: Rural areas in Clare have suffered losses of about 200 million Euro due to refusals over the past five years - an average of 40 million Euro per year.

* On a countywide basis the National Economy is losing hundreds of millions every year from refusals.

At the same time, Irish people are investing billions of Euro annually purchasing property abroad. The foregoing scenario is clearly contrary to the national interest.

The Draft Guidelines:
* While welcoming Minister Martin Cullen's positive statement of Government Policy in the Guidelines and previous positive statements by An Taoiseach, Minister O' Cuiv and many other local and national elected representatives, the daily experience of rural dwellers dealing with planning authorities leaves them in no doubt that radical steps are essential if the sea change promised in rural planning is to become a reality.

* The IRDA are happy to acknowledge positive aspects of the Guidelines, such as the definition of large towns (over 5,000), recognition of traditional linear development as distinct from ribbon development and other positive aspects.

Problem areas:
* The following aspects of planning in general are identified as causing the greatest difficulties throughout Ireland. They are either not addressed at all in the Guidelines or otherwise skewed in favour of Planning Authorities who are free to interpret them to continue to refuse as heretofore.

* Extraordinary powers of decision making by individual planners over peoples civil rights; entirely subjective opinions of individual planners resulting in blatant inconsistencies in decisions / refusals / grants of approval and binding subjective opinions over architectural details, size of house, colours of roofs, house styles, landscaping etc which rightfully are the prerogative of the applicant.

* Planners' powers to overturn reports by consultant engineers and architects relating to ground quality, percolation, house- design etc - applicants have nowhere to turn for justice.

* Applicants being passed from planner to planner due to staff changes resulting in different subjective opinions, creating extreme difficulties, costs, delays and hardship.

* Planners' demanding extraordinary levels of personal details from applicants.

* Planners have assumed roles of being Lord and Master and treat applicants accordingly.

* Planners binding decision on applicants `need' for housing.

* Planners binding subjective opinions on landscape issues leading to refusals.

* The Guidelines refer only to the Planning Authority - individual planners are not mentioned. However, in each and every case, the Planning Authority boils down to an individual planner as far as the applicant is concerned.

Recommendations:

* The role of the planner to be re-examined as a matter of urgency in open consultation with all social partners. Powers to be defined by agreement and published in the Guidelines and all County Development Plans.

* Powers to be seriously circumscribed.

* A request for a pre-planning meeting should be responded to positively and promptly.

* A sea change in the role of the planners to that of a provider of positive assistance on some technical matters such as health and safety, building regulations, guidance where requested or needed on other relevant matters to reverse the present authoritarian system.

* Planners should "deliver quality services with courtesy, sensitivity and the minimum delay..." in their dealings with members of the public. These and other aspects of Quality Service Standards are outlined in the Government Publication Principles of Quality Customer Service for Customers and Clients of the Public Service.

* Subjective opinion making by planners to be reduced to an absolute minimum.

* A speedy, easily accessible local system of arbitration / appeals must be put in place to resolve differences long before refusals are handed down.

* Planners should be instructed to advise applicants on what they need to do to obtain permission following a refusal.

* The needs and civil rights of the applicant are most important - planning is a service, not a dictatorship.

* Agreed changes in the role of the planner to be carried through to 3rd level Colleges where courses should change to comply.

* All planning courses in 3rd level institutions to be immediately reviewed in consultation with all social partners / stakeholders and a new approach / philosophy developed and agreed after public discussion.

* Irish accreditation to replace the RTPI system.

Non National Planners:

* Irish traditions in terms of community life, culture and history are neither acknowledged nor taken into account in individual planning applications. This is in spite of Government policy to the contrary and to Rural Proofing Policy.

* The situation, bad enough as it is at present with Irish Planners trained under a UK influenced philosophy of urban and town planning is exacerbated by the presence of so many non-national planners at local authority and Bord Pleanala level. Nationality itself is not the problem, but the fact that these planners are not obliged to have taken any course specific to the Irish situation serves to make an already bad situation worse.

* It is highly relevant that the British Government now considers it necessary to directly intervene in England's own housing crisis. "...planning regulations would be relaxed...some green field sites would have to be issued...massive building programme...2 million houses in the next decade" Deputy Prime Minister John Prescott, who has overall control of housing policy said it was time for a "step change" in the house building ...the planning system was "too conservative". (Observer 21/3/04)

Recommendation:

* All planners working in Ireland should have studied and be qualified in Irish history, culture etc. This is natural and just.

* All applicants should be entitled to examine the qualifications of planners dealing with their case and demand proper qualifications as a base minimum in seeking fairness and justice.

* All decisions / recommendations presented in writing by planners should carry details of qualifications held by the individual involved. The seriousness of the issues involved i.e. to grant or refuse permission to build a house and associated property and civil rights, demands openness and transparency at every stage.

* Titles such as Executive Planner, Chief Executive Planners etc should be supported by evidence of appropriate Irish and rural studies.

* All applicants should be entitled to have their cases dealt with as Gaeilge if they so wish.

Locals only:

* All locals only restrictions should go. The enforcement of these restrictions is regarded as totally unacceptable and unjust. (See attached paper locals only)

Sterilization of land:

* This restriction should go. It is regarded as unjust and unconstitutional by all rural dwellers.

Occupancy Clause:

* This restriction, where it is imposed, is regarded as unjust in all aspects. It should also go.

The three foregoing restrictions i.e. Locals Only, Sterilization and the Occupancy Clause, single out rural dwellers for different treatment under the Constitution and civil rights than urban dwellers. This is unsustainable and unacceptable in our democracy. All three are bound to face legal challenges at both national and EU level as time goes on with the potential for massive compensation claims against planning authorities.

An Bord Pleanala:

* Widely regarded as having an anti rural housing bias, evidence of refusals confirms this belief.
* The public are entitled to some process of redress against incorrect factual information in inspectors reports without having to go to the High Court. Currently the Bord is answerable to no authority in this respect.
* "Reasons must be given by An Bord Pleanala when the recommendation of an Inspector of An Bord Pleanala is overturned". (10% of cases). [Joint Committee of the Environment and Local Government - second report - November 2003}.

Recommendations:

* Composition of board members should be changed to include rural interests such as farming, rural dwellers, community and relevant social interests to achieve balanced representation. Only then can balanced decisions be arrived at.

* All planners employed by the board to deal with rural houses should have the same qualifications as outlined for local authority planners elsewhere in this submission. This rules out the sending of rural housing cases to planners outside the State.

The fact that so many single house applications are objected to reflects an urban view of rural Ireland, that houses per se are an affront to the landscape and attributes anti-social motivations to prospective house builders. A correct and balanced understanding of Irish rural history and population distribution is vital if justice in planning is to be achieved.

3rd Party Objections:

* While accepting the principal of the right to appeal, 3rd Party objections to single houses are totally out of proportion in Ireland. Singe houses do not pose threats to any 3rd Party on a scale similar to dumps, incinerators, industrial polluters etc. Potential dangers from septic tanks or to road safety are technical matters for local authority officials and are dealt with during planning applications. Other aspects such as of landscape, heritage, archaeology are also dealt with in the same way.

Recommendations:

* 3rd Party Objections to be confined to people living in close proximity to the site whose property or other rights can be proven to be put in danger by the proposed building. The current situation where 3rd Party objections can be made by anybody either in or outside Ireland to single houses is patently unjust and unconstitutional and widely abused.
* Criminal Offence: it should be made a criminal offence carrying stiff penalties to deliberately interfere with the planning process by way of fictitious, spurious, frivolous or otherwise false 3rd Party objections.
* The bona fides of objectors / letters of observation to be established before being accepted as valid by local authorities an An Bord Pleanala.
* Names of all objectors to be published in newspapers by planning authorities and An Bord Pleanala.
* Proxy Objections for reward should be made a criminal offence.

Landscape:

* In general, the official interpretation of the human presence in the Irish landscape causes immense problems for rural and would be rural dwellers.

* Positions are polarised.

* A hierarchal, judgemental set of principals skewed in favour of landscape over people and community life pervades official thinking on rural planning.

* This largely urban view generally translates into a presumption of refusal for rural houses. There is no level playing pitch and planners can refer to a whole draft of regulations / restrictions and pseudo authoritative designations by urban based consultants and heritage groups to support their subjective opinions. While social policy on community life continues to be ignored by planners, individual applicants cannot win.

* Regrettably, the Guidelines appear to do little this area to assist the regeneration of rural communities with new families and new houses. Planners can continue to refuse as before.

* There is no evidence that arguments in favour of community life or the traditional scattered or dispersed village carry any weight against the landscape philosophy described here.

* Example: Different landscapes allow for siting of houses in 'sympathetic' ways such as, hillocks, valleys, woods etc. However, in many coastal regions such as West Clare, which supported 10 times the present population 160 years ago, where the landscape is often flat and treeless, refusals average 50% + because each new house is clearly visible. This planning view is skewed in favour of total depopulation.

* The principal should be made in the Guidelines that a suitably designed and landscaped house can enhance virtually any (but not all) landscapes (exceptions to be agreed in consultation with local representatives). The Irish landscape housed 6.5 million people in the past. The current rural population - 1.5 million.

* Landscaping: Over proscriptive landscaping conditions should not be applied by planners. The rights of the prospective homebuilder to make these decisions should be respected.

Recommendations:

* A complete public re-examination of the human presence / landscape philosophy in consultation with all social partners and stakeholders. Irish history, culture and traditional population distribution to play a paramount role.

* The re-examination which is a matter of extreme urgency must start from a green field philosophical site.

* Outcome: The expected outcome will be a complete Irish planning philosophy on the totality of rural life as well as all other important factors of National importance such as the East, West population balance, high density living etc.

Interim measures:

* In the interim, planners should comply with Government policy in favour of rural community life.
* The IRDA should be given listed status in the Planning process. "Consideration should be given to prescribing additional organisations, whom would be likely to hold views contrary to those of An Taisce, in order that greater balance could be given to the appeals process". (Joint Committee Department of the Environment - second report - Sept 2003)

Specific Comments on Guidelines:
(By Page)

* Page1 - Change "and" to "or" (par.4)
* Urgent need to define `depopulation' in rural areas- no adjectives   to be used.
* Define `future needs' of rural communities as expressed by locals.
* Define `local circumstances' - should include school numbers - loss of services etc.
* Define `have regard' to Ministerial Guidelines.
* Page 5 - 1st par. Change `have regard' to `comply'.
* Page 7 - remove the word `modest' in 3rd Paragraph from the bottom.
* Page 10 - (1) Insert `non-residential' to qualify the phrase `development in rural areas' i.e. `non-residential development in rural areas'.
* Page 10 - Par. 7 - same as above i.e. `non-residential development to the right locations in rural areas....'
* Page 13- "Preserving the character of the landscape." Should include reference to people.
* Page 14 - (1) rural populations to match 19th Century patterns.
* Page 20 - Farmers should be allowed to build a holiday house to rent as a business enterprise.

* Page 22 - 4 last paragraphs - restrictive - no scope for resettlement or social housing - remove the page altogether.

* Page 23 - `development plan definition of need' - unjust

* Page 23 - `Landscape ...assessment'. There is no objective method of landscape assessment (see CAAS report)

* Page 26 - extra domestic traffic from new house using existing exit should not be reason for refusal.

* Page 27 - seeking personal information on applicants background is unjust

* Page 27 - Personal circumstances have no place in a just planning system.

* Page 33 - (2) power to An Taisce

* Page 35 - 2nd last paragraph - locals only - no room for resettlement or social housing.

* Page 36 - Explain justification for last paragraph (d).

* Page 37 - 3rd Paragraph - wide open for subjective opinions leading to refusals - unjust.

* Page 38 - 2nd last Paragraph - leaves local authorities open to compensation claims?

General Comments:

The final Guidelines should be covered with a clear and unambiguous statement of Government policy and legislative framework and with firm instructions to Planning Authorities and to An Bord Pleanala to implement in full the spirit and letter of the law. In this context, rural

dwellers will be looking to County Managers to announce publicly the intentions of their Administration to comply. It should also be noted that a number of Administrations in different counties have already declared that the Draft Guidelines offer nothing by way of changes in planning and in some cases are even more restrictive than their County Development Plans.

* The Guidelines should be based on a clearly expressed recognition by the Government of the right of those who wish to live in a new single rural house to do so.

* Visually vulnerable: Laws designed to restrict housing in areas designated visually vulnerable or similar, do not apply equally to urban and to rural dwellers. A comparison between the East coast and the West coast demonstrates the truth of this. Both coastal regions are equally "beautiful". However, in the thickly populated East, huge stretches of coastal areas are completely residential with houses in one time small villages like Killiney, Dalkey or Howth fetching millions of Euro. In spite of this massive building development these areas are still considered the most upmarket and desirable places to live. By comparison, in the West where

depopulation has hit hardest, the same urban dwellers who live in luxury on the East coast are the most vociferous in denouncing Western dwellers for "destroying" the landscape with their scattered houses. Rural dwellers are no longer accepting this situation where blatant discrimination in civil rights is enforced on behalf of urban dwellers by the planning regime.

* New Business Enterprises: The Guidelines should be positive towards the establishment of new small rural business enterprises. Existing businesses should be allowed to intensify. Small family enterprises are essential for sustaining community life.

* The Guidelines should acknowledge the need for relativity between the size and scale of the proposed house and the size of the site as well as greater choice in positioning the house in the site.

* The Final Guidelines should clearly state that all sites are eligible for consideration for planning permission irrespective of their previous planning history including past refusals by local authorities and/or An Bord Pleanala.

* Rural Living: All grants of permission for rural houses should include advice on the sounds, odours and general activities associated with normal agricultural life, which are to be expected in rural areas. City dwellers have to accept delays, traffic-noise, ambulance sirens etc. as a fact of life.

* Costs of applications: Planning Authorities should be conscious of, and concerned for the costs of making planning applications. Planners should be proactive in trying to keep costs to a minimum on a case by case basis.

* Social Housing: Policies of restricting Social Housing to villages and towns is creating a two tier society with serious long-term implications. Social Housing should be directed also to rural areas where full integration is the norm.

* Refusals in this generation resulting in clearing out the rural people will result in future invasions from wherever demanding and obtaining services and the right to build. In the meantime rural people suffer.

* Road Traffic:
`Probability of accident' principle should be applied instead of automatic refusals vis-à-vis speed limits, line of sight, etc. An extract from the submission by Michael Leahy, Charted Architect and Town Planner, states "In regard to traffic safety, again planning authorities should be asked to spell out very clearly the criteria that will be used in assessing whether or not individual planning applications represent a traffic hazard. In this regard some planning authorities will apply the same sight distance criteria to a single house discharging on to a

very small rural back road as they would to a large housing estate discharging on to a national secondary route within a 30 mile speed limit area. (I have in fact experienced this). Clearly the extent of traffic hazard is dependant, not just on sight distance but on the probability of accident, which is determined by the number of trips being generated by a particular proposal (which in the case of a one-off house would obviously be very small) and also the volumes of traffic on the road which is be accessed. Planning authorities should be obliged to carry out proper traffic assessments of each application on the basis of probability of accident rather than imposing a blanket restriction. As a former local authority planner myself, my training as a planner involved the methodology of assessment of probability of accident - something which is well understood and not very complex. A requirement for say a 90mtrs sight distance measured 4.5mtrs back from the road edge would effectively preclude any applications in those areas most in need of regeneration i.e. the areas classed as of dispersed settlement pattern in the west of Ireland as shown on Page 16 of the Draft Guidelines. By simply applying excessive traffic safety standards planning authorities will have a clear route to frustrate the Guidelines if they so wish and while such may not be the intention of the officers within the planning system, individual planning officers are, in my experience, perfectly capable of behaving in this manner". (End of Extract).

* Traffic Regulations (cont'd): Equality of treatment should be given in planning between new agricultural exits and new domestic exits onto roadways.

IRDA Special Recommendation
National Rural Planning Monitoring Committee.

* The establishment immediately of a Rural Planning Monitoring Committee along the lines of the Group Water Schemes Monitoring Committee is proposed. This latter model put in place to oversee developments in water schemes', water quality etc works extremely well and has statutory powers including direct appeal to the Minister.

* Because of the turmoil over rural planning outlined in this submission and the radical steps proposed to deal with the situation for the good of the country, a Monitoring Committee could play a critical role in the immediate and long term future.

Composition / Structure:
* In outline, the Committee would be representative of all social partners, the Dept of the Environment, County Councillors and other stakeholders in the planning process. It would have a national and county structure.

Principles:
* It would adopt the principle that it is of profound importance to the social, cultural and economic life of Ireland where people live and where they have lived in the past. It would respect the constitutional and democratic rights of all citizens.

National:
* On a national basis, it would monitor the development and introduction of an Irish Planning Philosophy.

Local:
* Locally, it would monitor the implementation and compliance with Government Policy by Planning Authorities. It would play a critical role of arbitration in disputes between applicants and local authorities. Appeals to An Bord Pleanala could become cases of last resort.

* It would monitor actions of local authorities and individual planners to ensure all their decisions were legal.

* Overall, it would be a recognition of the essential role and right of the people of Ireland to a direct say in how planning is organized on behalf of and in favour of present generations while giving due consideration to future needs.

Information
Irish Rural Dwellers Association

The Irish Rural Dwellers Association was formed in May 2002 by

Declan MacPartlin	PR North Connaught Co-op
Pat O'Rourke	President, ICMSA
Liam O'Cuinneagain	Director, Oideas Gael
Cathal O'Searcaigh	Poet
Cathal McGabhann	Retired CEO< Udaras na Gaeltachta
Senator Labhras O'Murchu	Director, Comhaltas Ceolteoiri Eireann
Dr. Jerry Cowley, TD	Chairman, Rural Doctors Group
Chairman, St. Brendans Village	
Dr. Seamus Caulfield	Archaeologist, Ceide Fields Project
Ruairi O'Conchuir	Project Manager, Rural Action Project, Kilrush
Marcella Tiernan	Chairman, National Executive of the ICA
Sean Hannick	Chairman, Council of the West
Maurice Harvey	Chairman, Rural Development, ICMSA
Jim Connolly	Chairman, Rural Resettlement Ireland
Seamus Breathnach	County Councillor, Galway Co. Council
Jerry Lundy	Sligo Community Devbelopment Forum
Marion Harkin, TD	Member Dail Eireann
Tom Lynch	Acting Secretary, Kerry
James Doyle	Representative of the IFA
Sean O'Baoil	Director, Udaras na Gaeltachta
Con Hickey	National Chairman, Western Committee, IFA

The common bond between all these people and the organisations thay are associated with is the love of our country and its people and in particular the love of our rural cultural heritage.

The issue that brought them together was planning for houses in rural areas. The issue has reached crisis point in Ireland. The traditional townland or dispersed village settlement pattern which has existed here for over 5,000 years is under attack from the palnning regime. The right of people to choose where to live are gone as well as any concern for rural community life or our cultural heritage. The individual has no hope in achieving justice in planning, but by uniting against the unjust planning reigme we will win.

The IRDA support the efforts of County Councillors in their statutory duty of formulating planning policies which reflect the concerns and constitutional rights of all citizens. The role of professional planners is to implement policies not to dictate them. Rural dwellers will not be forced into urban areas.

County Development Plans are critical—they set the rules for years to come. Now is the time to join the IRDA and form support groups in your county to have a real voice in your County Development Plan.

Already, Kerry, Wexford and some other counties have shown the way with major changes introduced in the County Development Plan due to the local efforts of the IRDA.

Application Form
Irish Rural Dwellers Association

You can make a copy of this form or cut this page out and post it.

Application Form

(BLOCK CAPITALS PLEASE)

Full Name
_____

Address
_____

_____

Telephones
_____

Fax
_____

email
_____

Declaration

I declare my support for the main aim of the IRDA and, by becoming a member, to assist in the development of the association in my own area, in the county and at national level.

Main Aim:

To unite all rural dwellers and people of goodwill towards rural Ireland and in the context of peaceful, multi-cultural co-existence in the common cause of ensuring, by legal and constitutional means, the growth and maintence of the dispersed village, sraid bhaile or street village and the clachan or nucleated (clustered) village.

Copies of the constitution and legal status of the IRDA are available on request.

Signature   Date
_____

Annual Membership €20

Post to:

Acting Secretary, Jim Connolly
Irish Rural Dwellers Association,
Kilbaha, Kilrush,
County Clare.
Tel: 065–905 8229.